THE

THE MARRIAGE
ADVANCE

15 ANSWERS TO QUESTIONS MEN WON'T ASK

Bryan Van Slyke | Jody Burkeen

The Marriage Advance

Authors:

Bryan Van Slyke
Founder of www.manturity.com

Jody Burkeen
Founder of www.manupgodsway.org

DBA Burkeen Ministries Inc

Cover design by: Chelsea Van Slyke
Start your next cover design @ www.sistapits.com

ISBN: 978-0-9839288-5-0

CONTENTS

ACKNOWLEDGMENTS

Bryan Van Slyke

After dating for nearly 6 years, I was finally able to marry the love of my life in 2006, Chelsea. Each year since then has been a wonderful journey of not just learning about ourselves, but really learning about each other and understanding the plan God has for our marriage. Because of the grace of God and my wonderful wife, I was able to put these powerful words and testimonies together. Thank you Chelsea for pushing me to become a stronger husband and better man of God each and every day! I love you!

Jody Burkeen

I want to thank my Lord and Savior, Jesus Christ, for saving me from my own destruction and sending me my helpmate, Nan. Thank you for loving me, standing beside me, and never giving up. When you are by my side, I feel as if I could take on the world! I look forward to growing old with you! I pray our marriage will help others see that "till death do us part" is kind of cool! Love you with all my heart.

INTRODUCTION

By this point, you've already won her heart and you've already stated your marriage vows. Congratulations, that was a huge step in your life.

For some of you reading this that moment may have been few months ago, and for others that moment may have been years ago. Whatever relationship timeline you are on, it's important never to forget the reason why you got married and it's even more important never to forget your vows.

But I get it; life gets busy and can get hard at times. Things come up, mistakes happen and the history of your relationship is shaped as time continues to press forward. The ongoing timeline of your marriage continues, and, in some cases, so does the growth of your frustration over certain things your wife has done or said over the past months or years.

We wrote this book because we understand things happen in marriage. Both Jody and I, Bryan, have been married long enough to know how little things that happen in everyday life can turn into massive issues that bring marriages to a screeching halt. Both of us have been there and both of our marriages have been able to work through them.

Here are a few things we think might be going on in your marriage right now:

She disrespects you in front of your or her family.

She continues to do that one little thing that drives you absolutely nuts!

You have been married for some time and still haven't had sex or you feel there is an extreme lack of sex.

She's always asking for your attention.

These are just a few quick ones off the top of our heads, but it's easy to see how one or even a couple of these combined can start to really affect your marriage in a negative way.

It's not difficult to notice these issues starting and forming, the hard part is figuring out a way to resolve them. And resolution can't begin until you're prepared to talk about them and learn how to overcome them.

That's where we hope you will find this book effective. This book, as the subtitle suggests, is meant to provide insight and helpful answers to questions you keep thinking but aren't able to ask yet.

Here's the problem: if you're unwilling to ask someone for assistance in your marriage or talk to your spouse about your heart, your marriage timeline will look more like the one below than what you stated in your vows.

-An issue arises in your marriage.

-You notice it and stay silent.

-The issue only gets worse and you do nothing.

-You never ask for help. You never mention it to your spouse.

-The issue grows. Divorce seems to become a reasonable option.

Since both Jody and I went down similar paths earlier in our marriages, we understand the possibilities in yours and we know how you're feeling. We know why it feels as though staying silent is a better idea than opening up to someone.

What we both discovered though is that the timeline mentioned above doesn't have to be your story! By the grace of God, a hard slap of humility and the love of friends, we were able to bring back the timeline from when we won our wife's heart and when we spoke our vows. That is the timeline you need to get back to and stay on! That is the timeline to maintaining real life in your marriage.

Trust us; silence and divorce will be much more difficult than simply humbling yourself to someone safe and working on resolutions. It's possible!

You'll find that each chapter in this book is meant to address one question we feel might be on your heart but you won't bring yourself to ask anyone about it. We hope and pray that you take these questions and restoration options seriously. Some may apply to you, some may not. Some may apply to a friend or co-worker and now you'll have a direction to point him in. We would encourage you to read through the entire book once, and then reference it in the future as certain questions or issues may arise within your marriage again.

Don't back down from your marriage!

Believe that God has great things planned for your marriage!

Find questions. Take necessary action. And keep fighting, men!

Bryan Van Slyke - Manturity.com

Jody Burkeen - ManUpGodsWay.org

CHAPTER ONE

LEARN WHAT RESPECT MEANS TO YOU

By: Bryan

My wife didn't know the importance of respect, I didn't understand how to tell her and things just got worse.

QUESTION

Hey man, how can I get my wife to respect me?

ANSWER

You must understand God's definition and your definition of respect first!

RELEVANT VERSES

"However, each one of you also must love his wife as he loves himself, and the wife must respect her husband."
-Ephesians 5:33

"Do nothing out of selfish ambition or vain conceit. Rather, in humility value others above yourselves."
-Philippians 2:3

"Teach the older men to be temperate, worthy of respect, self-controlled, and sound in faith, in love and in endurance."
-Titus 2:2

What Is Respect?

What is respect? Although that is a very valid question that I think every man could attack and answer, I think there is a much more critical question. How do you define respect? How you personally define respect is what I really encourage you to discover in this chapter. If you can search through your past experiences with family, friends and your wife to discover your definition of respect, you will change the way you look at yourself and your marriage.

Every man has a built in desire to be respected, a deep need to be wanted and accepted. This need might have first presented itself on the playground in middle school. It may have come up when you desired to be good at certain sports so that you would be picked for a team. It might have started when you desired to be good at chess or another game so that you could fit in with a certain crowd. It may come across vain or selfish, but the deeper need was to be respected and accepted. We all have our own story and here is some of mine.

My Personal Story

I always wanted to go back and blame my pre-marriage counseling for some of my early marriage problems, but then I remembered that I was in my early twenties and I thought I already knew everything about life and marriage. And just like the important information we'll discuss in the chapter on sex and intimacy, I seemed to completely miss the necessity of understanding respect. I had no idea how I defined it, how to receive it from my wife and how to let her know how to show respect to me.

For the first few years of my marriage I didn't have an understanding or definition of respect for myself. Sure, I felt the deep need to be respected, but I never defined it. There were times when my wife would "call me out" in the middle of a crowd or around family and I'd just stand there dumbfounded. *What to do? How do I respond?* The carpet would be pulled from beneath my feet and all I could do was lay there. I'd lie there staring up at the ceiling wondering why I ever got married and why my wife hated me so much. What I came to learn was very important though, my wife didn't hate me at all, but she was disrespecting me. The bigger realization that came from these early experiences was that neither of us understood respect or disrespect. She didn't know the importance of respect and I didn't understand how to tell her, and things would just get worse.

As many more of these types of situations took place over time, I began to remove myself from our marriage more and more. She began to ask me why I didn't pursue her anymore. She would wonder why I didn't put my arms around her with deep love and emotion. Where were the flowers that I used to get her? I didn't feel any desire to take her out anymore. She was crying out for love, but I was lost in a sea of disrespect. The truth was I had no desire to show her love. Something had to change or, as I mentioned in the timeline at the beginning of the book, I knew our marriage would end way too soon.

You're going to start to realize in the coming chapters the importance and advantages of attending a marriage class. As a quick side note, you should seriously pursue and attend a marriage class or conference every year. The reason I am now a firm believer in this mindset is because of the first experience my wife and I had when we finally attended one. The first class my wife and I took with similar aged couples was "Love and Respect", by Dr. Emerson Eggerichs. It was through this video and workbook series that both my wife and I started to understand our own issues with love and respect. They gave amazingly general examples of love and respect from their own marriage and provided powerful testimonies from people who had already taken the course. Through these examples, we started to explore and define our own definitions of love and respect. This book and video series changed everything in our marriage and I'd highly recommend you take the course and read the book with your spouse as well. You can find more information about how to love your wife in the chapter on sex and intimacy.

The Importance of Understanding Disrespect

Let's keep digging further into your personal definition of respect. I want you to consider the times and moments when you think you have experienced disrespect. This could have happened when you were growing up, it could have happened more recently at work and it most likely happened in your marriage already.

Here are a few of my own experiences with disrespect and some scenarios you may be able to relate to:

How do you feel when you go to work all day and come back home to find that nothing has been done that you had specifically asked to be done?

How do you feel when you walk in the door after a long day of work and your wife immediately starts asking you where you have been and what you have been doing?

How do you feel when you have a great idea or direction to go at your work or in your marriage and nobody listens or cares?

How do you feel when you accomplish something great or complete something challenging and your wife doesn't seem to care or take notice of it?

There's a very good chance we've all encountered these types of scenarios in our lives. We have all had to deal with some form of rejection or disappointment. It's important to remember that we also feel disrespect in these moments, little moments when all you wanted was to be noticed and praised, but instead you were turned down or off. From these moments though, we can start to figure out what respect means to you. You learn from these moments because they pierced your heart. They most likely made you angry or frustrated.

They most likely made you shut down your heart. As much as you don't like to think of these moments, they will be where you learn the most about yourself and how you can help yourself and others in the future.

I will go ahead and share my top five things that respect means to me and then you can take some time to write down your top five. This process of clarifying your personal definition of respect will make a huge difference to you and your marriage.

Here are the top five ways that I define respect:

TRUST

I want my wife to trust me. Whether I am home alone or out with my buddies, I want her to know that I am all for her and her alone. I want her to know that she can always trust me and that she has nothing to worry about. We will fully dig into this topic in the coming chapter, "Women Other Than Your Wife".

WORDS OF APPRECIATION

I want my wife to use words that say how much she appreciates what I do for her and for our family. I want her to tell me things like, "Thank you for your hard work," and, "I appreciate the efforts you take to keep our family safe." I even appreciate the simple ones that offer appreciation for taking out the trash, picking up the kids or doing chores around the house.

WORDS OF AFFIRMATION

I want and desperately need my wife to affirm me; I long to know that she is attracted to my appearance and my heart. I want to hear her say things like, "Good job," after a completed project or task. I need to hear her say, "I'm proud of you," when the time is right and calls for it to be said.

COMFORTABLE WITH SEX

I need to know that my wife wants me sexually. I want her to know that I only have eyes for her and that she is my desire. I want her to be comfortable with my "subtle" advances towards her. I want her to love my pursuing her and I want our sex life to be amazing and something we both look forward to.

EFFECTIVE COMMUNICATION

I don't want my wife to call me out in a crowd or talk down to me. I can't stop her from acknowledging my mistakes or setbacks, but I can ask her to approach me at a more appropriate time and then discuss what's on her heart. I want her to encourage me and continue to work with me, even if I make wrong or bad decisions. I want her to be on my side through any form of communication or issue.

These are my top five areas of what respect means to me. These areas have all been reviewed with my wife throughout our nearly 10 years of marriage. She knows what respect means to me, and she goes out of her way to make sure these needs are met. I do the same thing when I choose to love her in the ways that she needs to be loved. Again, take some time to really dig into the coming chapter on sex to learn more about love and intimacy.

Our Challenge to You

So now I want to challenge you to write down what respect means to you. On the next page write down how you define it. How could you help your wife understand you more? Explore different areas and examples of disrespect from your own life, build upon my five areas that I shared and dig into the deeper aspects of your heart. DO NOT take this process lightly and get started now.

You can do this in two ways:

Use the 5 bullet points below to list your definitions or feel free to list your points in a separate journal.

The ultimate goal is to dig into your heart and write it down.

1)

2)

3)

4)

5)

Once you have successfully completed this challenge, I'd encourage you to do three more things to help you and your wife grow in your love and respect for each other.

The first is to read the book or attend the class *Love and Respect*. As you start to get a better handle on how you define respect, you are going to want to better understand how to love your wife.

As you embark on reading or watching this information, I challenge you to share your list of what respect means to you with your wife and even adjust them to be more exact.

The last thing I want you to do is pray for your marriage in specific terms of love and respect. Pray consistently that God will teach you how to define respect and how to express those definitions to your wife. Pray that, as you understand respect for yourself, you will learn the value and need of learning how to love your wife. If you take this chapter as seriously as it needs to be taken, you will not only change your marriage, but you will change as a man. I know you can do it!

CHAPTER TWO

THE
DEAL WITH
PORNOGRAPHY

By: Jody

The perverted beauty of a woman on a computer screen kills the love we are to be sharing with our wife.

QUESTION

Hey man, does watching

porn affect my marriage?

And can I watch it with my wife?

ANSWER

Yes and No!

RELEVANT VERSES

"Flee from sexual immorality. All other sins a person
commits are outside the body, but whoever sins
sexually, sins against their own body."
-1 Corinthians 6:18

"It is God's will that you should be sanctified: that you
should avoid sexual immorality; that each of you should
learn to control your own body in a way
that is holy and honorable."
-1 Thessalonians 4:3-4

"...'you shall not commit adultery.' But I tell you that
anyone who looks at a woman lustfully has already
committed adultery with her in his heart."
-Matthew 5:27-28

The Problem

Every man remembers the first skin mag or skin flick they saw. You're over at that one friend's house where there were no rules, no parents at home after school. The dad had a stack of nudie books somewhere "hidden" in the house. They also had the satellite TV on which you could see the naked images behind all the "white" noise if you pointed the satellite in the right direction. No matter your first experience, it's still stuck in your memory, burned there forever.

Now, I'm not trying to make you drum up that image and cause you to stumble, but I am trying to make you realize the problem with our lust goes way further back than the current internet porn. It's a problem with the heart.

The verses in Psalms 119:10-11 says, "I seek you with all my heart; do not let me stray from your commands. I have hidden your word in my heart that I might not sin against you."

Many "Christian" men haven't picked up a Bible in years and have nothing but sin and deceit hidden in their hearts. Without an understanding of what God considers sin, we justify our sin.

We rank it with other sins, such as, "Murder isn't as bad as porn," or, "A pedophile is worse than adultery." Most of the time we rank our sin with someone else, such as a friend who is getting a divorce or relatives that you know are sinning. It's easy to compare ourselves to others, but our example is in Christ. He is the model we should be conforming too. But all too often men are not following Christ, but the flesh.

As a born-again believer, my lustful thoughts should begin to die with acceptance of Jesus as our Lord and Savior and the repentance of my sins. I wish it were instantaneous, but it's what we call in "Christianese" sanctification. It's a process through which I am trying to be better than I was yesterday in God's eyes. And this is a lifelong process.

The underlying issue with all lust is sin! Period! But why do we continue to sin? Well, it's because we don't see sin how God sees sin. God sees all sin as evil and due punishment. And so should we!

Personal Testimony

My addiction began at the age of 12. I found a nudie book and masturbation at the same time. Since I had never been told what either was I explored the possibilities of both on my own. That addiction grew with me through high school and all the way to marriage.

Somehow, I had talked my wife into believing it was good for our marriage. We began to watch porn movies together and that led us to going to strip clubs together. It seemed all well and good until we became parents then Christians.

After our salvation in 2003, my wife was able to turn her desire for porn movies off. She no longer believed we should be watching those kinds of things. Well, my desires didn't stop when hers did. I started watching internet porn.

Internet porn led me to stay up later than my wife, seeking time alone with a computer more than time with my wife. (Side bar- How sick is it that we desire a woman on a screen more than the real thing in the bedroom?) And so began some big problems for me sexually.

My desires in the bedroom were that my wife should do the things that were on the computer screen. This led to a lack of desire because, at the same time, I never wanted to degrade my wife like that. It also caused another problem. I became the "minute man". Not something I was real thrilled with. But, unfortunately, that is what happens to many men.

You see, what happens when watching porn is that most of the time it's done in secret and hoping that no one catches you. It's not like you sit down with a candle, have a glass of wine, and enjoy the moment. No, it's done for speed. Get done, don't get caught, and hide the evidence as fast as possible. And this is where the problem comes in. We become Pavlov's dog. Pavlov was a famous scientist who took a dog and when he fed the dog he would ring a bell at the same time. As the dog ate, he salivated. Pavlov did this multiple times. He would feed him and then ring the bell.

After a while, Pavlov stopped feeding the dog and would just ring the bell. What he found was that the dog would still salivate. Even without food. The dog had become so accustomed to the bell being associated with food that even when no food was there, but only the bell, he still salivated.

This is what happens to most men, we associate a nude woman's body with masturbation and speed then when we get in the room with the real thing, we lose control, thus making us a "minute man".

Porn Kills Love

The addiction of porn does much more than ruin your sex life, it kills the heart and the heart is the place where love starts.

Slowly but surely, the love you have for your spouse fades. Our minds get so wrapped up in a fantasy world that we forget the reality that our relationship with our spouse takes work. We may fall in love, but in order to stay in love we have to put forth effort. And with porn in the mix, it begins to ruin us. It begins to make us not love anymore. That is the power of the sin of lust, immorality and envy.

The perverted beauty of a woman on a computer screen kills the love we are to be sharing with our wife. The one flesh God gave us, but the addiction of pornography takes over and kills the true love in our life.

The Cure

Admit you have a problem!

The first step is always admitting it. You and I are good liars, so good we convince ourselves into believing a lie. That lie is "I need it." We don't need porn! So start by being honest with yourself; look in the mirror each time you are under pressure and say, "I have a problem."

Confess the problem!

I would suggest you start with a man you can trust. Let him keep you accountable and be open with him! Only honesty and accountability with a partner will work. You need to give him permission to ask the tough questions, see your phone, and even your computer.

You need cyber help!

Once the process of confession has begun, and repentance is sought, you need to put barriers between you and the porn. Get porn blockers on all of your devices and for your home. Keep your home computer in an open location where anyone could see your activities. This will help fight the temptation of wanting to get on it again. Most blockers have accountability built into them, so if you stray or fail, it will send an email to your accountability partner. This is a huge deterrent. For a complete home porn blocker, go check out: http://www.buctools.com. This is a tested system that we highly recommend.

Confess to your spouse!

I believe it takes time to overcome the addiction to porn. There will be ups and downs and that's why I suggest you start with a man. But eventually you need to be honest with your wife. Share with her the struggles you have had with porn; be open and honest with her just like you were with your accountability partner. Let her ask you tough questions and see your phone and your computer too! From this day forward, let her keep you accountable too.

This is also a good place to share with your wife your sexual desires and needs so you can both come to an understanding of what you expect and what she expects. Then keep working towards a happy medium. My wife and I did this and she was there to help me with my desires, but also I got a gauge of what she needed as well. It has worked well for us.

Take it one day at a time!

The addiction to porn is something that just won't go away on its own and it won't be quick. Spend daily time in the Word and in prayer. Learn to take your thoughts captive and replace them with scripture. Learn to "lust" for your wife and not a computer screen. Pursue your wife when you get the urge to view porn and focus on her, not just physically, but emotionally and spiritually!

Our Challenge to You

If after reading this chapter you admit that pornography is a threat to your marriage or you know of a brother who might be struggling, we would challenge you to begin a 30-day fast from porn.

Make a choice to do this challenge along with reading the book, or make it a point to start when you complete this book.

Do your best to journal your thoughts, actions, accomplishments and failures. And remember, take one day at a time and do it alongside a fellow brother if possible. Accountability is powerful and we'll talk more about it in an upcoming chapter.

CHAPTER THREE

THE MULTIPLE LEVELS OF INTIMACY & SEX

By: Bryan

Intimacy doesn't start in the bedroom;
it starts at the beginning of each day,
and continues into every interaction
you have with your wife.

Trust must be established and maintained
in your marriage in order to have an
amazing and long-lasting sex life!

QUESTION
Hey man, how can my wife and I have a better sex life?

ANSWER
Stop thinking about the physical part of sex and start learning the value of intimacy outside the bedroom.

RELEVANT VERSES

"Husbands, in the same way be considerate as you live with your wives, and treat them with respect as the weaker partner and as heirs with you of the gracious gift of life, so that nothing will hinder your prayers."
-1 Peter 3:7

"Therefore if you have any encouragement from being united with Christ, if any comfort from his love, if any common sharing in the Spirit, if any tenderness and compassion, then make my joy complete by being like-minded, having the same love, being one in spirit and of one mind. Do nothing out of selfish ambition or vain conceit. Rather, in humility value others above yourselves, not looking to your own interests but each of you to the interests of the others."
-Philippians 2:1-4

"The wife does not have authority over her own body but yields it to her husband. In the same way, the husband does not have authority over his own body but yields it to his wife. Do not deprive each other except perhaps by mutual consent and for a time, so that you may devote yourselves to prayer.
Then come together again so that Satan will not tempt you because of your lack of self-control."
-1 Corinthians 7:4-5

A Personal Journey toward Intimacy

I have been honestly seeking after the heart of Christ for almost five years now. It has been powerful and the most intense time of my life. I have enjoyed the challenge of getting to know and understand the life of Jesus and His Word. I have also been challenged in my experiences with other people and have shifted from a mindset that says every man for himself to how does Christ want me to impact the life of other men? That has certainly taken some courage, but it has also forced me to be more intimate with other men—intimate in the sense of getting to know them on a deeper level of the heart, you know, beyond the latest scores or work drama. Since God has broken into my emotional side and ripped it into pieces, I know that is what is needed for many other men.

Jesus now requires me to be more open about my emotions, my pains, my confusion and more. He encourages me to go to deeper emotional levels, levels that I never saw my own father go to and levels that I never allowed myself to experience early in my marriage. These new levels of emotional intimacy with Christ and with other men of God have allowed me to open up to higher levels with my wife.

If you can set aside some of that manly pride and open up to some of your emotions, you'll be amazed at how much it will impact your sex life.

These next steps on this topic may not be easy for some of you, but they do require your full attention.

Where Does Sex Start?

A great sex life with your wife does not start when you are naked and under the sheets; a great sex life starts with deep emotional intimacy (at least after the honeymoon phase of the marriage). Emotional intimacy includes things like a deeper level of communication, a deeper level of care and a deeper need to truly meet the needs of your wife. Intimacy, in short, requires a lot of work but it is well worth it! A great sex life starts at the beginning of every day and continues into every interaction you have with your wife.

What Intimacy Looks Like on a Simple Level

When talking about intimacy on a simpler level, we must review the needs of your wife. What does she like? More importantly, what does she dislike? And I'm not talking in terms of her favorite food or favorite restaurant or bands, although knowing those types of things does hold some weight when it comes to taking her out on a date or trying to figure out what kind of gifts to give her. I'm talking about holding her hand, putting your arm around her, choosing her company over your cell phones, sending little text messages throughout the day and so on. It's those small things that are more than likely simple to perform either daily or at least weekly, and they are ways that impact her on a more intimate level.

Step up! Text your wife now or leave her a little note today to get things started!

But maybe you're thinking that those kinds of things are dumb or useless. Maybe you're thinking that she's just being needy or trying to waste your time. If you do happen to embark in this type of thinking, I would challenge and highly encourage you to STOP right now! I would also challenge you to pray about these types of incorrect feelings and ask God to show you simple ways you can be intimate with your wife each day. Pray that He will show you the little opportunities and that you will have the courage to take them. You're not going to like this truth, but your marriage is not about what you think your spouse needs, it is about what she says she needs. It is about understanding what the scriptures say your wife needs and craves from you. When it comes to what you need, be sure to seriously review and accept the challenge in the earlier chapter on respect.

If you will focus more on the needs of your wife than your own, you'll truly start to tap into the emotional intimacy that could lead to a great sex life.

After being married now for almost ten years, I wanted to share with you a few **simple options** that have worked for my marriage and could potentially work for yours as well. As you create these scenarios, keep track of the ones she really likes and the ones that she does not. Also, be on the lookout for her ideas or what she would like to see you do. You might see her become more open to sharing those types of things as you start to engage in more actions of intimacy.

1) Leave her a little note in a different place in your bedroom or house each week. As she goes through her day, she will randomly find them and a little spark of intimacy will pop off!

2) Take the initiative and set up a date night. While you are on the date, take some time to pull away from the useless conversation and let her know how much you really love her and appreciate her. Let her know how much you liked that dress she wore a few days ago or let her know how much you appreciate her going to work or taking care of the kids. These little comments will go miles!

3) Give her a day off from the responsibilities. Let her go out with some friends or family or just let her go out

and do whatever she has wanted to do. While she's out and about, take the initiative in cleaning up the house, taking care of the kids or getting some of those outstanding 'honey do' items completed.

4) Be more physically intimate with her in a non-sexual way. Hold her hand the next time you go out driving together. Put your arm around her the next time you are at Church or sitting beside her. Invite her to sit next to you on the couch one night and just hold her close. These subtle physical touches will lead to more intense physical touch!

5) Be more engaged with her. The next time you get home, put away your work emotions and phone, and just be with her. Take interest in her day or her work activities. Talk to her about her goals and dreams. In other words, just shut up for once and truly listen to her!

Brothers, take the next couple of weeks and try some of these ideas in your own marriage. Be intentional about doing them each day or week. As the spiritual leader of your home, it is your responsibility to initiate these actions. Make these tasks and make her a priority! We'll talk more about how you can be a stronger spiritual leader in a coming chapter.

What Intimacy Looks Like on a Deeper Level

The ideas and challenges I mentioned previously were simple tasks that every man should be able to handle. The next few areas involve intimacy on a deeper level. They involve events that may have already happened; they involve your level of intimacy with Jesus and your willingness to go to a deeper level. Remember this, the more willing you are to set aside your pride and selfishness the greater chance you have at amazing sex with your wife.

The first place we have to start is your relationship with Christ. Why? Well, because that is when it all changed for my life and my marriage. Once I truly acknowledged the need to have Christ at the center of my life; I was able to connect with Jesus, other men and my wife on a much deeper emotional level. It changed everything. If you're past the honeymoon stage of marriage and wondering what happened to your sex life, I challenge you to review your level of intimacy with Christ. Are you praying often and watching for the answers and guidance? Are you reading His Word and trying to live for Him in all that you do? He is not seeking perfection; He is seeking your willingness and faithfulness to try hard every day. Are you willing to do that?

Seek a more intimate relationship with Jesus and you'll be amazed at what it will do for your marriage. You'll be amazed at what it will do for every aspect of your life!

Putting Christ first will teach you the value and need of putting your wife first in your marriage. -Van Slyke

The next few areas to consider on a deeper and more intense level are trust and commitment. Let's keep digging in, men.

Build and Maintain Trust

Trust is essential to a strong emotional bond with your wife and for an amazing sex life. One of the main reasons my wife and I struggled with sex at the beginning of our marriage was due to trust. She was still dealing with issues from her one of her old boyfriends and I was still trapped by pornography from college. We both had issues in areas that we couldn't figure out or understand, and neither of us would admit to them or talk about them. Those two issues brought on our first few talks of divorce. I was frustrated that I was taking the heat from the past guy's mistakes and she was hurt that I needed to see women other than her for pleasure. Let me make a note here that you must dig into the chapter entitled "Women Other Than Your Wife", which goes into great depths about your relationships with them.

I'll be completely honest, getting to the point of explaining why we still had these issues and were allowing them to impact our marriage was not easy. Her explanation came out only after I told her I couldn't take the confusion anymore and needed the truth or I was moving on from her. My explanation came out after getting caught by her one night on my computer. Neither of these moments was very pretty, but they were exactly what needed to happen in order for our dark areas to be resolved and for us to truly trust each other.

Through time, forgiveness and a lot of faith in God, we now both love and trust each other more than ever. And because we were both willing to go to those rarely touched places and deeper emotional levels, we can now talk about anything in a controlled manner. We do this because we are always seeking Christ in our marriage, which allows the trust in our marriage to stay strong.

What about you? What is the state of trust in your marriage? Are you concerned that your wife is doing things or talking to other men behind your back? Does she have any reason to be concerned about your actions or you doing the same thing? Trust must be established and maintained in your marriage in order to have an amazing and long-lasting sex life!

Maintain Commitment

How committed are you to your marriage? Do you even remember the words you spoke when you said your vows to your wife? Those simple words were some of the most important you've ever spoken to another human being. Those were not just words, they were promises and they represent your deep level of commitment to your wife and your marriage. Those words are supposed to represent forever. Remember, the good and the bad; in sickness and in health; till death do you both apart? Every wife wants and desperately needs to know that you are committed to her. She needs to know that the women at your work or the woman at the grocery store checkout has a minimal impact on you. She wants to know that, if things go wrong or if the budget gets tight, she can look to you for resolution, not avoidance. She wants to know that she can go to you with anything and trust your heart. She needs to know that you are fully committed to her. She needs to feel that from you often.

And going back to what I said before, a strong and committed relationship with Jesus will help you keep your marriage this way. Strive to show her daily, weekly, monthly and yearly that you are committed to her and the great sex will continue for years to come.

Our Challenge to You

As if I have haven't given you enough to think about and try in your marriage already, here are a few quick and final follow-up ways to help you have a more fruitful sex life.

1) Keep your relationship with Christ active, engaged and intimate.

2) Review and apply the **simple options**, and examples I gave you earlier in the chapter.

3) Pray daily for your marriage and for your sex life.

4) Review and resolve any open issues related to your past or deeper levels mentioned later in the chapter.

5) Become a full-time student of your wife! Continue to find out what she loves and continue to do those things for her!

CHAPTER FOUR

SPIRITUAL LEADER

By: Jody

If God is calling you to do something,
no matter how farfetched,
He will see you through it!

QUESTION

How can I become the spiritual leader in my home?

ANSWER

Slowly!

RELEVANT VERSE

"But I want you to realize that the head of every man is Christ, and the head of the woman is man, and the head of Christ is God."
-1 Corinthians 11:3

The Problem

As you walk into Churches today, you see many of the programs and ministry outreach efforts performed by . . . women. In some cases, these same women are also the head of the household, raising kids, paying bills, and sometimes bringing home the bacon. The biblical model that God gave us—that men should be the leaders in the Church and home—is not being followed by many Christian men today.

Countless married Christian men have become spiritual sissies. These men have their tail between their legs, and their wives have them by the collar. Many of these men have allowed their wives to call all the shots, and they just follow them around like a lost puppy waiting for the next treat. In many cases, it's not because the wife wants to act this way, but because she doesn't have the choice because her husband simply isn't stepping up.

Don't get me wrong: I am not being a chauvinist with these statements. Women have a major role to play in God's kingdom and the home, and they are equally gifted in many areas of ministry. As a matter of fact, the Bible gives us many examples God used mightily for His kingdom. But, unfortunately, this has become the stereotypical view of Christian men today: whipped like dogs and too frail to stand up for their God, their family or their marriage. Men need to bronze themselves and Man Up!

Personal Testimony

When I was married, in 1990, my wife was far more mature than I ever thought about being. Some might say she still is. But since I became a Christian, in 2003, our roles have reversed.

During the first thirteen years of our marriage, my wife was raising me. I mean that in the sense of the way you raise a child. She always had to mold me, scold me, and hold me just like a kid. And I came to the point where I actually liked it. The day before I got married, my mom made my bed. The day after I got married, my wife made it. I had just gone from one mom to the other. I was the biggest sissy around. My wife was my mom, not my soul mate. She spent many years training me to become a man. It didn't work too well because that isn't the biblical model, and I think over time she finally stopped trying and just let go.

In the early years of our marriage, when people asked us about having kids, I would jokingly say, "She has to raise me first." What I later realized was that it wasn't a joke. Not a good way to be a biblical husband.

Husbands, love your wives, just as Christ loved the church and gave himself up for her to make her holy, cleansing her by the washing with water through the word, and to present her to himself as a radiant church, without stain or wrinkle or any other blemish, but holy and blameless. In this same way, husbands ought to love their wives as their own bodies. He who loves his wife loves himself. After all, no one ever hated their own body, but they feed and care for their body, just as Christ does the church— for we are members of his body. "For this reason a man will leave his father and mother and be united to his wife, and the two will become one flesh." (Ephesians 5:25–31)

After I accepted Jesus as my Lord and Savior, I began to read what the Bible says about being a good Christian husband. What I found was that I wasn't even close to the biblical model, and neither were most of the men I'd met in Church. But reading about what kind of husband I needed to be and actually doing it were two different things. I had thirteen years of bad habits to get rid of and an old, comfortable routine.

I had a wife to convince that I had changed, and I had to close my ears to Satan telling me I couldn't do it. This, so far, has been the biggest challenge for me in my Christian walk.

In my marriage, I had made a lot of mistakes. I had let my wife down more than once. So for me to start trying to assert my newfound "spiritual head of the household" attitude . . . well, it was going to take a long time, a lot of prayer, and actions that were much different than what I had shown in the past. As she has always said, "Actions speak louder than words."

My wife had spent our marriage providing the majority of the income. She had moved up in the ranks as a pharmaceutical saleswoman in one of the largest companies in the industry.

She was successful, beautiful, and confident, and she was fast becoming the number one salesperson in the company. This was something I was proud of but also very jealous of. The jealously part is something I didn't bring up very often.

But after having kids, my wife's job began to suffer. We had a full-time live-in nanny while we both worked, but the thought of leaving her children with another woman became just too painful for my wife and began to affect her attitude at work. On top of all this, for the first time in our lives, we were listening to the Holy Spirit and allowing Him to direct our lives. What He was telling us to do was a hard pill for me to swallow.

God was telling my wife she needed to stay at home with our kids. This was not something I felt we needed to do, not because God wasn't talking to me too, but because I was not ready for this kind of change. All I was worried about was the money, the lifestyle, and having to step up and be the man of the house.

If God is calling you to do something, no matter how farfetched, He will see you through it. It won't be without trial or without error, but He will see you through to the end.

"Consider it pure joy, my brothers and sisters, whenever you face trials of many kinds, because you know that the testing of your faith produces perseverance. Let perseverance finish its work so that you may be mature and complete, not lacking anything." (James 1:2–4)

The Fix

This is kind of obvious but... JESUS, JESUS, JESUS!

Get into the Word! Daily! Make sure you spend time with God the Father through His son Jesus Christ! This is the only way you can become the man that God has intended you to be!

Next, learn to pray for and with her. This was one of the biggest things that helped change my marriage and established me as the spiritual leader. Once you start having conversations through prayer with God, it's easier to have them with your wife! Don't let the sun go down without praying for and with your wife!

Our Challenge to You

Start reading your Bible daily, pray daily, and make changes in your home slowly.

More specifically, make a choice to wake up early the next 7 days and pray for guidance on how you can be a better Spiritual Leader for your family, your friends and your co-workers.

Let your wife see you becoming the man God is calling you to be. Don't force it!

CHAPTER FIVE

RESOLVING TRUST & INSECURITY ISSUES

By: Bryan

If you don't know what love looks like to your wife, take her out on a nice date or walk on the town and ask her how you could love her better.

Maintaining trust in your marriage is essential.

QUESTION

Hey man, how can I stop my wife from asking me what I think of other women or getting jealous when she thinks I'm looking at another woman?

ANSWER

Recognize whether she has past issues or if you are truly getting distracted and not recognizing it.

RELEVANT VERSES

"Ask and it will be given to you; seek and you will find; knock and the door will be opened to you. For everyone who asks receives; the one who seeks finds; and to the one who knocks, the door will be opened."
-Mathew 7:7-8

"...the Lord delights in those who fear him, who put their hope in his unfailing love."
-Psalm 147:11

Personal Testimony

Trust is a vital component of a strong and long lasting marriage. Without trust, a marriage will only fall into a deeper pit if not addressed. Without trust, insecurities from both spouses will only increase and become more negative.

The years leading up to my marriage consisted of college. Three years of spending time with a bunch of guys; it was an all-male school that was anything but affectionate or trustworthy. I was also about 6 hours away from my fiancée, which made it very hard to see each other. We would be lucky to see each other every other month. Once our schooling was complete, we were married three months later. I had no idea what I was getting myself into.

After spending years around rough and tough males, I now spent most of my time with this beautiful, soft spoken, love driven woman. She was wonderful, but I didn't have a clue how to love her. I had just spent the last three years not being affectionate and not worrying about feelings and emotions. My life over the next couple of years would change dramatically.

It was just two years into my marriage and I found that my wife was always coming to me for attention. She would say things like, "Why don't you just come up to me and put your arms around me?" "Why don't you look at me the way you look at that Hollywood actress or the girl at the grocery store?" "Why don't you just want to sit and cuddle rather than have sex?" These type of questions started coming at me from her and I didn't understand why. I mean if I didn't need that kind of stuff, why did she?

She needed them because that is how I show love to her. That is what she needs in order to feel loved and cherished. By doing those small but important things for her, she could maintain a stronger trust in me and in our marriage. Those types of actions also made her feel much more secure in the relationship.

What I learned and questions for you to consider:

Are you affirming your love to your wife often?

Are you making your love known to her around other people?

Are you making a real effort to maintain her trust?

Let's take a closer look at each question and see how it applies to your marriage.

Are you affirming your love to your wife often?

Any good book on marriage will tell you that your wife has a constant need to be loved by you and for connection with you. There is never a point in your marriage where her love tank is completely full and you can stop showing her love. It is the exact same need that you have when it comes to respect, as we discussed at the beginning of the book. There is never a point where you want your wife to stop thanking you for all your hard work and for what you do for her and your family. Personally, I can't hear that enough.

So with that all said, are you affirming your love to your wife often? Can you even remember the last time? Do you even know what type of love and affection your wife likes to receive? These are all vital marriage questions and I need to you consider each one and answer them directly. As hard as it may be, this is where real change can start to take place when it comes to trust and insecurity issues.

If you don't know what love looks like to your wife, take her out on a nice date or walk on the town and ask her how you could love her better. If you can't remember the last time you did something that showed love, hurry up on that first idea on a date. As you ask those questions, it's important to shut your mouth and open up your ears. Do whatever you can to understand and retain the critical information that is coming from her. And whatever you do, don't take offense at her answers. If you're asking her to open up her heart, it may come across as painful to you, but it's exactly the type of information you need to hear. Once she shares her heart, let her know that you understand and that you'll make a bigger effort to meet her needs and fill her love tank.

Are you making your love known to her around other people?

I once worked with a couple where the wife desperately wanted her husband to show her some affection when around family or friends. She desperately needed to know that, even in large crowds, she was her husband's main focus and priority. In the end, he couldn't understand the need and refused to take any action. It is exactly that kind of attitude that will lead to more distrust and insecurities in your marriage.

More recently, my wife brought up a similar situation. Every year we find ourselves going home for the holidays. Although we love spending time with family, it's really easy to get caught up spending time with everyone else and forget the needs of your spouse. Well, this happened to us and it didn't go over well.

Through this experience in particular, my wife felt left out and unloved. She felt that I was making everyone else a priority over her. And even though I didn't mean for it to come across that way, that's exactly what it looked like to her. Since we have had about 4 years now of rebuilding our marriage and making it stronger, she was able to share her emotions on the topic that very night. I didn't enjoy it and took some offense at it, but, as I said earlier, I shut my mouth and listened to her heart.

She opened up and said that she felt lonely and unloved due to my constant visiting of everyone but her. She asked that, for the rest of the weekend, I would be more aware of her and her needs rather than everyone else's first. At first, I'll admit, I was a bit offended by her emotions, but I had to dig deep and remember that these were emotions from her heart. By doing what I did, she felt alone and insecure. These moments of the heart are not the time to take offense or shut down, they are moments to listen and take action on. By the end of the conversation I told her that I understood and I would be more aware of it for the remainder of the weekend. That is exactly what I did and we left it at that. The issue was resolved and we were able to move on. This, of course, will work both ways.

Are you making a real effort to maintain her trust?

Finally, it's important to make an effort to maintain the trust in the marriage. As I said above, after learning of my wife's needs, I took action on them the very next day and we were back to doing great again. Now, to take things a step further, it's important to remember those same needs in the future when we are in similar situations. I mean it's what we would expect of her if the roles were reversed. Right?

Notice I didn't say that maintaining trust and love in the relationship would be easy. In fact, it's not very easy in the world we live in today, but it is achievable and it is worth it. The all-important vows you spoke to each other on your wedding day should be a reminder for the both of you.

Some simple ways to maintain trust involve knowing what each spouse needs. It's making sure that once you know what those needs are you take action on them often. If you have a fear of forgetting, you might write down the needs and enter them into your phone calendar or one of your other personal calendars. It may feel like a chore to you, but you must remember how those specific actions make your wife feel. You must not forget how important those things are to her. Again, you wouldn't want your wife to forget what things you need, like sex and respect. Right?

Our Challenge to You

Maintaining trust in your marriage is essential. It is something you and your wife need to feel often. You can see just from a few of my personal examples that you are not alone in this type of walk and that you can already relate with some of your own stories.

What about your own stories? What about the last time you visited family and had a large argument with your wife? What about the last time you were at the mall and your wife accused you of staring at other women? Your recent situations in your marriage will tell you exactly where you need to take action. Your recent fights or disagreements will give you some powerful insight into where you need to work on your marriage and where your wife may feel insecure. And with that knowledge, you need to take action on those areas today!

Here are 5 things to consider that will help you improve trust and insecurity issues in your marriage.

1) Are you being honest with your wife? When she questions you about another woman, are you being honest about your actions towards her? When she thinks she catches you looking at another woman, are you being honest about whether or not you really looked at her with lustful eyes?

2) Are you ready to ask her what she needs and are you willing to listen? The next time she comes to you needing to be held or loved, will you be aware and ready to meet that need, regardless of your personal opinion? The next time she calls you out in a situation, are you ready to confess to it and prepare to make the necessary changes?

3) Are you aware of her past relationships? As her husband, it's critical that you step back and

consider her past relationships. Were any of her past boyfriends very deceptive and untrustworthy? Does she still hold those emotions deep in her heart and aim them to you? Was her father one to be trusted? Consider her relationship to her father as well and that will help you in knowing what she needs and may not like.

4) Are you letting her know your needs as well? I realize I've spent a lot of time on recognizing your wife's needs and desires, but there is a benefit to it as well. If you are willing to take the time and listen to what she needs, she will be much more willing to take the time and listen to your needs. If you take the initiative to make the relationship better by seeking to know what love means to her, she will be more likely to want to know what respect means to you.

5) Are you praying for your wife and with her? Praying with and for your wife is one of the most powerful things you can do for your marriage. Prayer allows you to speak blessings and love over your wife without having to do it directly to her. It also allows you to have open discussion about your wife and marriage with Jesus. As you share your heart with Him, He will lovingly speak wisdom and truth back into you like you couldn't imagine.

Are you ready to take a stand against lies and the evil that is trying to get in the middle of your marriage? Well, you should and I encourage you to do it today! Review the many questions in this chapter and find out which ones really apply to you and which ones will really improve your marriage.

More specifically, pick 2 of the 5 considerations listed and start applying them to your marriage today. Make yourself notes or check back each day to make sure you're actively seeking to improve these areas.

Don't wait another day to re-build powerful trust!

CHAPTER SIX

HOW TO OVERCOME THE LITTLE THINGS

By: Bryan

Those little annoyances in marriage may
be small at first, but if unresolved,
they will turn into
bigger and worse issues.

QUESTION

How can I make sure the little things in our marriage don't become really big issues?

ANSWER

No matter how small the issue might be, you need to discuss it and seek resolution with your wife as soon as possible.

RELEVANT VERSES

"Fools show their annoyance at once,
but the prudent overlook an insult."
-Proverbs 12:16

""In your anger do not sin":
Do not let the sun go down while you are still angry,
and do not give the devil a foothold."
-Ephesians 4:26-27

"Love is patient, love is kind. It does not envy, it does not boast, it is not proud. It does not dishonor others, it is not self-seeking, it is not easily angered
it keeps no record of wrongs."
-1 Corinthians 13:4-5

What qualifies as a little thing?

My wife and I had only been married for a few months when the little things started showing up in our marriage. Instead of looking at these things as "just little things", I came to realize they were subtle differences between her and me, you know those things that you grew up doing one way and she grew up doing them completely different. Remember I said different, not wrong.

One of the first little things or differences in my marriage showed up in our kitchen. To be exact, it all had to do with our kitchen sink and the counter space beside it. You see my wife grew up with a dishwashing machine and I grew up as the dishwashing machine. I did have two older sisters whom I traded off the nightly duty of doom with, but I still had to participate. So where does the problem come in? Well, where do you put the dirty dishes?

Yes, the dirty dishes were a really hot topic when my wife and I were first married. Actually, I just got the look the other day because I still mess up on occasion and totally by accident. Since my wife grew up with a dishwasher, she always put the dirty dishes in the sink. Since I did not, I grew up putting the dishes on the counter beside the sink. They had to go next to the sink, since we used the sink for washing. So, as you can imagine, this little thing became a big deal, as my wife could not understand why I always put the dishes on the counter. Things were about to change.

At first, I had a hard time understanding her logic and why I needed to change my ways. Instead of thinking about the common sense reasons, I thought she was trying to control me. I wanted to do it my way, but needed to remember that we were now a team and we had to work together. I eventually understood her reasoning because we did, in fact, have a dishwasher and it really didn't matter enough to damage our marriage.

It honestly took a couple of years to get really used to the change, but I did manage to adjust my habits. I didn't always get it right, but she knew I was trying and gave me large amounts of grace. And just to add a little comedy to it, at one point she put a sign on the counter beside the sink that said, "No Dishes Here." It was pretty funny, but deep down I knew she was serious. We were both able to laugh about it and I continue to try to keep the dishes in the sink. Pray for me, guys!

It may have been a little thing, but it was a big deal to my wife and to the long-term success of our marriage. There could be a lot of these things that come up early in marriage and it's important that you recognize the value of reviewing and resolving them quickly. If you can do that, it will make the process much easier as little things pop up later in marriage.

Take a second and think about the little things in your marriage. Some might be funny and some might be a really big deal. Now that you have one or two, let's keep going.

The Little Things That Can Make a Much Bigger Impact

Let me take a moment to explain another little difference between my wife and myself. In my wife's family, her father was the spiritual leader when she was growing up. He led the family in devotion time, he pushed everyone to get up on Sunday mornings to get to Church and he encouraged a strong relationship with Jesus Christ. In my family, the role was the opposite; my mother was the spiritual leader. She was the one who led the charge for attending Sunday service and school every week and even pushed for my sisters and me to have a Christian education. It wasn't that my father was not a good man; he just wasn't raised to lead in that area and in that way.

What did that type of upbringing mean for our marriage? Well, on Sunday morning she would be waiting for me to take the spiritual lead and, you guessed it, I'd be waiting for her to take the spiritual lead. This did not make for much of a spiritual walk early in our marriage.

For the first few years of our marriage, we struggled with this indecision and confusion. It wasn't until our marriage started to take a nosedive that I learned about my role as a husband and the importance of spiritual headship. I was fortunate enough to have a brother from our Church tell me about the role I needed to take in marriage and share some of his personal testimony about leading his family. You can dig further into this important topic of mentorship and accountability in the chapters titled "Accountability" and "Spiritual Leader". We spent a few nights together talking about the importance of initiating the spiritual leadership in my family and that it was my responsibility, not my wife's. I was the one who should have been leading my wife to Church each week. I was the one who should be have been leading a devotional and encouraging a strong relationship with Jesus. This was the exact type of push and direction I needed in my life.

Are you initiating spiritual headship and leadership in your marriage? I realized through this process that something as little as who led the spiritual charge when you were growing up could have a huge impact on your marriage. As you review your own situation, I would encourage you to treat this little thing as a very important topic in your marriage. Start leading and making a big deal of it today!

Our Challenge to You

How to Approach Resolutions to the Little Things and Differences in Your Marriage

Prayer

Praying should always be your first step to finding resolutions in your marriage. Ask God to reveal the areas where you are having small issues with your wife. What areas or things are annoying you over and over? What little changes could mean big improvements? Continue to pray about these things and allow God to speak to you about them.

Make a List

When you have thoroughly prayed about those things, take some time to sit down and make a list of them all. This list is very important and is critical to fully understanding each area. I want you to review them all carefully and continue to pray over them. There might be some that will require a change in you! Yes, you, not your wife. If you noticed, both of my examples required a change in me. I didn't see the need at first and I put up a little bit of a fight, but God showed me where I needed to change. He could be asking you to do the same thing in your marriage. Try not to fight against this idea, but trust that God has a great plan for you and for your marriage. It will be worth it.

Talk to Your Wife

Not all of these steps will be easy, but this one is going to sound like the worst or at least appear the worst. You must approach this step with caution, care and love. First, let her know that you have been praying for your marriage and reviewing areas where you, not her, could improve and become a better husband. Let her know that there have been some things that have been bothering you in the marriage that you wanted to pray about first. Then let her know about some areas where you are going to make changes in your attitude and in the way you do some things. Once reviewed, carefully and lovingly discuss some of the little things that she does that might bother you. Let her know why they bother you and talk to her about ways the two of you could work towards a slight change and resolution. Since you have already reviewed your issues and your changes, she should be more willing to work with you in these other areas. Lastly, and most importantly, pray with her about all of these things discussed. Notice I didn't say pray directly for the areas she needs to change, because that would make you lose every piece of ground you had gained at this point. Just invite God into the moment and into all of the little areas discussed and allow Him to work on your marriage in powerful ways. Be open and willing to hear what He has to say.

Don't let the little things go unresolved for another day!

PRAY WITH HER TONIGHT!

Resolution is absolutely possible if you're willing to accept the challenge above!

CHAPTER SEVEN

IMPROVE YOUR COMMUNICATION

By: Bryan

Instead of making my wife
and marriage the first priorities,
I was making them the last ones.

QUESTION

Hey man, why does it seem so hard to talk
to my wife sometimes yet so
easy to talk to anyone else?

ANSWER

You must understand that great
communication is critical to your marriage,
but that you have an enemy
always at work against it.

RELEVANT VERSES

"That is why a man leaves his father and mother and is
united to his wife, and they become one flesh."
-Genesis 2:24

"My dear brothers and sisters, take note of this:
Everyone should be quick to listen, slow to speak and
slow to become angry."
-James 1:19

A Perfect Beginning

I find it fitting that in the few days leading up to writing this chapter on communication, my wife and I were terrible at communicating. Notice that I didn't use the word surprised, I used the word fitting.

The miscommunication wasn't even about anything important. I think the biggest issue we had was figuring out where to eat and then the confusion of whether or not we were going to eat in or get the food to go. The disagreement was no less ridiculous, but these are the exact types of fights or disagreements that can multiply over time and end a once good marriage.

There were a few things I needed to be aware of and keep in mind though; my wife already wasn't feeling well and she ultimately needed to get some rest. With that in mind, I kept my temper and my peace, and after she'd had a nap for a couple of hours she apologized and we made up. This is how small disagreements or miscommunications need to be handled, regardless of which spouse is on the giving or receiving end; there ultimately needs to be some perspective of what else might be going on, which could assist in a quick resolution. If these things don't happen, the small things, as I talked more about in the previous chapter, will all group together and the end will seem in sight. There is no need to let it go that far!

Since we all have experienced pain and have struggled in the area of communication in our marriage, I want to share a few specific areas where I struggled and sought resolution with my wife.

My 3 Personal Areas of Struggle

- Sharing My True Feelings

- Listening

- Working as a Team

Sharing My True Feelings

I want to be very honest with you; although I have gone through these pages and poured out my heart multiple times, I have never been a man who easily shares his feelings. I have learned through a lot of prayer and training that I can express feelings, thoughts and emotions on paper much better than I can in actual conversation. However, after writing now for a few years, I have become much better and more willing to express my emotions face to face with my wife or another person. It might be a process that you should consider in your own life.

I was terrible at sharing my heart for the first few years of my marriage. I wanted to be tough, I wanted to be a "yes man", and I didn't want my wife or anyone else to know how messed up I was inside. This pattern of thinking and my relentless pursuit of keeping my heart in a box led to multiple breakdowns with my wife.

I can remember at least two occurrences early in my marriage where I finally showed my true heart. The first time it happened, I sat in a room and fought against it until I finally broke down. I finally gave in to all of my emotions in front of a trusted man and I couldn't stop them. As embarrassing as it felt, it was an unbelievably freeing moment. I finally shared my heart and was able to discuss my deep issues with a trusted friend. This process then led to me sharing my heart with my wife. These were things that I had kept bottled up for a few years, but, regardless of my fear and her reaction, they were things that needed to be said. They were not easy to say in front of her, but they did lead to making some needed adjustments and more honesty in our communication.

To this day, I try not to hold too much inside. I either let my wife know that there's an important issue that we need to discuss or I call up a trusted brother. Either way my heart is able to get it out and it makes a huge difference in my marriage and manhood.

What about You?

Are you really good at keeping your emotions, thoughts, needs or desires on the down low? If so, I would encourage you to change your habits now! The best place to start is by opening up your heart to your pastor or a trusted brother in Christ. Become a man who is strong enough to seek a resolution to his issues because that is true strength! Once you are able to discuss some things with another man, move on to being more open with your wife. If you fear that step, start making that a daily prayer. Learn how to talk about issues quickly and work out resolutions. These major adjustments in communication will change your marriage forever!

Learning to Listen

Have you ever been around a group of men talking about marriage or relationships (they could be about personal or general things, it really doesn't matter)? When we are willing to share stories and examples, we also like to add a resolution to every problem. In other words, we go through a process of listening, but then we also have to offer some kind of advice or personal recommendation based on our own experiences. As men, our general goal is to fix everything. Well, this may work around a group of guys, but have you ever tried this method with your wife? As she proceeds to share her struggles with you, you are probably listening but more than likely trying to come up with a solution. And this, my brothers, can be a dangerous path. Let me share from personal experience.

It was roughly a year or two into our marriage when I was driving home from a long day at work. My wife was working full time in a corporate setting and, as I came to find out, had a very bad day. She called me and proceeded to tell me all of the reasons why her day was so bad. "So and so said this about me." "Somebody decided to say something they shouldn't have and I couldn't believe it." After some time of her telling me all of these things, I started picking away at them and offering solutions. Here is how you can handle that situation and here's what you could say to that person. As I went on with my solutions, she interrupted me and said that she didn't need to hear my resolutions she only needed me to listen. She needed to get her frustrations out to someone and that someone happened to be me.

I learned from that moment, and from many experiences since then, that my wife just likes me to listen to her. She doesn't always need a resolution. She doesn't always need my opinion. Sometimes I just need to shut up and listen and then there are other times when she just needs to know that someone does care for her and that she can turn to me in times of need. The best answer in this case, and in many others, was to just listen to her in the moment and then hold her close when we were together again that night. It's always important to remember and maintain good perspective that she isn't mad at you, she's mad at the situations at work. Every mature husband must keep this type of perspective in these situations.

What about You?

Are you able to just listen to your wife and focus on her needs? If not, I would encourage you to just simply shut up and listen to her. When she comes up to you after a long day or a rough situation, do your best to ask minimal questions and just listen. Now, if she does ask for your advice, keep it short and sweet. And, of course, always try to be on her side with your advice. Other than that, open your ears and hold her close. Let your wife know that, among all of the chaos of life, you can always be her solid ground.

Communication and Teamwork

One of the first big mistakes I made in my marriage was agreeing to something my parents asked me about before talking to my wife about it first. This happened on multiple occasions before I finally understood that my wife and I were a team and we had to work together. I had to go to her, just as she needed to come to me, before any large decisions or planning would take place. I wish I would have learned this sooner.

The first few times this happened was around the holidays. I'm convinced that every couple comes to realize how crazy those first few years of holidays together are in marriage. Where do you go? Which parents do you visit? Which ones do you visit first? If both families have parties going on at the same time, which one do you attend? All of these questions have come up over the years, but that last scenario is where I fell into trouble the most. I'd get a phone call out of the blue from my mother about the holiday dinner schedule and just go ahead and agree to all of it; later that night I'd get home and share this schedule with my wife. This, of course, either led to her saying the same thing about her family or she would ask why I didn't talk to her first about it.

From those interactions there would come big disagreements. They typically included a lot of yelling, very little listening and absolutely no teamwork. We needed to get ahead of this process and fast! What I didn't realize at the time was that I wasn't putting my wife first. I wasn't cleaving (united as one) to her or being one with her as it calls out in scripture. Here, take a look at the verse again.

"That is why a man leaves his father and mother and is united to his wife, and they become one flesh."
-Genesis 2:24

Instead of making my wife and marriage the first priorities, I was making them the last ones. Something had to change.

I have come to learn a very important response in my marriage and it goes something like this: "Let me discuss this with my wife first and I'll get back to you with an answer." Now don't get me wrong, men, this isn't a way to belittle yourself or an attempt to take away your freedom; this is a way to show others that your marriage is very important to you and comes before whatever is being asked or thrown at you. And to put the little voice in your head to rest, yes, your wife should be doing the same thing with you. I always take this approach in my marriage now when getting invites from friends, family or even work (if possible). You and your wife are a team and need to learn to function as a team! One basketball player can't win the game on his own, but he can win if he communicates and works together with his team.

What about You?

Are you really good about making plans and then letting your wife know about them last? If so, I encourage you to change the game today! Once you find out what's going on with something, make it a priority to consult with your wife before you commit or give a final answer. She may pretend like it's not a big deal, but she'll appreciate the fact that you thought of her and put her first. Great teamwork in your marriage will always produce great and long lasting communication.

Our Challenge to You

1) Take some time to think about past communication issues in your own marriage. Are there any that are unresolved or need to be discussed? If so, take some time to pray about them this week. Once a few days have passed, seek to review and resolve them with your spouse.

2) Make it a goal to no longer hold in your emotions or feelings. When issues do come up in the future, seek to get them resolved as soon as possible. Remember, if you feel you can't talk to your wife about the issue, step up and speak to your pastor or trusted brother first. Then move on to your wife. And always be careful to keep your tone and approach loving.

3) The next time an issue does arise; try to take an extra 30 seconds to respond. Use your better understanding and mature perspective to realize whether she is mad at you or something/someone else. Decide whether she needs an answer or if she just needs you to listen.

4) When your wife says something and you think that you heard it incorrectly, be sure to say back to her what you think she said. This works great when you don't quite understand what your wife is trying to tell you. Repeating back to her in a loving way will allow her to confirm what she told you or clarify it. This is a great tool to use and can be used by both of you.

5) Pray about your communication with your wife and be consistent in seeking resolutions to issues. Prayer can be both with her and while you are alone. The important thing is to keep God invited and involved in your communication with your wife.

CHAPTER EIGHT

IMPROVE YOUR PRAYER LIFE

By: Jody

A rich and fulfilling prayer life
is essential to your spiritual growth.

QUESTION

How can I have a meaningful prayer life
and what does it look like?

ANSWER

Practice makes perfect and let's look at Jesus.

RELEVANT VERSES

"One day Jesus was praying in a certain place. When he
finished, one of his disciples said to him, "Lord, teach us
to pray, just as John taught his disciples."
-Luke 11:1

"God has surely listened
and has heard my prayer."
-Psalm 66:19

The Problem

Religion has taken over in the Church. We have lost the ability to have a relationship with Jesus and it is affecting every aspect of our walk.

Our marriages are crumbling and our families are being torn apart. Because of this division in the home, it is killing the Church as well and when the Church starts to fail so does the country! Why is this? I believe it is because of the lack of prayer or at least the right kind of prayer.

I travel the nation speaking about the complacency of Christian men in their home and in their Church. I ask this question at every seminar: "How many men here are reading in their Bible and praying daily?" Only about 6% raise their hands. And we wonder why everything is going to hell in a hand basket!

Bible reading and prayer should go hand in hand. It's the quality time that you and I have with the Father that makes a difference in our lives.

Many men have no clue how to pray. So they choose not to pray at all.

I love the Apostles! All of their flaws are right in the Bible for us to see, but also all of their hearts. Look at what the Apostles asked Jesus to teach them. "One day

Jesus was praying in a certain place. When he finished, one of his disciples said to him, "Lord, teach us to pray, just as John taught his disciples," Luke 11:1. Really, pray? Why not how to walk on water? Or raise the dead? And yet they ask Him how to pray!

Wow! My guess is that they saw the power that was in Jesus every time He went to pray. They saw that His power came from prayer! If that had been me, I would have wanted Jesus to show me how to raise the dead. That would be an awesome party trick!

But, no, they wanted to know how to pray! And therein is the problem with us! We don't pray nor do we try to learn how to pray. How so does the saying go, "Practice makes perfect." Even with prayer that statement is true.

Stop praying popcorn and 911 prayers, and start looking for God in your quiet time and in your heartfelt prayers!

Learn to pray!

My Testimony

Early in my Christianity, I began to write a prayer journal. At first it seemed, well, a little feminine. I believed a journal was something little teenage girls wrote in and hid under their beds but, reluctantly, I began to write one.

Day after day I was writing down my prayers to God, just like I was saying them. And after months of writing, I had three or four books filled up. But something I noticed more than anything was not much had changed in my life. I wondered why.

So I went back and started reading my older prayer journals. One after another I read them. What I discovered was that I had become a Pharisee!

"And when you pray, do not be like the hypocrites, for they love to pray standing in the synagogues and on the street corners to be seen by others. Truly I tell you, they have received their reward in full." -Matthew 6:5

Although I wasn't standing on a street corner praying, my journals had become my street corner. I was writing just to be writing, not really praying, just uttering words on the pages of my journal.

I also saw that I spent a lot of time praying for myself, not others. I call them "the whoa and why me" prayers. I was so focused on myself that I began to also become selfish even in my walk. I expected people to look at me, serve me, and help me with my problems instead of relying on God and Him helping me with them. So it became about me instead of Him and a very ritualistic process. In other words, I had a dead prayer life!

Solution

Fast Facts: Although 90% of Americans say they pray (60% say they pray every day), the ways they pray vary significantly, according to pollster George Barna. Two out of three unchurched Americans (63%) pray regularly, but only one out of three (34%) is sure that praying makes any difference. In contrast, nearly 70% of the "born-again" respondents think God personally responds to their prayers.

Among those who pray:

• 95% express gratitude to God

• 76% ask God to forgive particular sins

• 61% make specific requests of God

• 12% pray in tongues

- *National & International Religion Report*

If you are like most of us, life has seasons, and sometimes lacks consistency. I cannot think of anything more important than intimacy with our Heavenly Father. *"It is good to be near God."* (Psalm 73:28) Nearly fourteen hundred verses in the Bible talk about prayer. A rich and fulfilling prayer life is essential to our spiritual growth.

Here is how I encourage you to pray

Timing, find yours

Morning or night, it doesn't matter, just find your time. "Therefore be alert and of sober mind so that you may pray." (1 Peter 4:7) I am a morning person and that works best for me. It is a great way to start the day.

Be disciplined about your schedule—and stay with it! *"Be faithful in prayer."* (Romans 12:12)

Just start with a few minutes a day and eventually you will see it becoming a lot more!

Get alone privately

"But when you pray, go into your room, close the door and pray to your Father." (Matthew 6:6) Get away from the distractions of your life. Leave your computer, phone, iPad etc. in the other room! Stay out of bed and in a room without a lot of distractions and noises.

Pray, then shut up and listen

"Be still, and know that I am God." (Psalm 46:10)

Contemplate His presence. Take a moment to realize that Almighty God, the Creator of the universe, is waiting to hear from you! *"God has surely listened and has heard my prayer."* (Psalm 66:19)

Once you have taken your time to talk with God, just sit back and listen! Wait for Him to reply. It won't be an audible voice, but it will be that quiet voice of God. If you aren't listening, you will miss it! *"Listen carefully to the Lord your God."* (Exodus 15:26)

Talk with the Father, the Son and the Holy Spirit.

When you pray, to whom are you praying?

Speak to all three members of the Trinity. Tell God you want to be His man.

Tell Jesus you want to be more like Him. Ask the Holy Spirit to fill you with God's power.

Ask Him to open your spiritual eyes to see and your spiritual ears to hear what God is saying.

Pray with A.C.T.S.

A.C.T.S. is another great tool and an easy way to remember key elements of prayer. My prayer time has improved dramatically since I started using it. It's simply prayer in four parts:

Adoration - *"Praise be to God!"* (Psalm 68:35) Tell God how much you appreciate Him. Express your love for Him. Praise His power and majesty. This is a great way to begin your prayer time. Sometimes I watch the sun rise, and praise God for the beauty of His creation. You should never run out of praise. *"How awesome are your deeds!"* (Psalm 66:3)

Confession - "If we confess our sins, he is faithful and just and will forgive us our sins and purify us from all unrighteousness." (1 John 1:9) Tell Him where you have fallen short. Be specific. I thank Him for the forgiveness I have in Christ, and ask for help and strength to turn away from future temptations.

Thanksgiving - Always *"glorify him with thanksgiving"* (Psalm 69:30). You have plenty of reasons to be thankful. Thank God for His love, His faithfulness, His patience and a million other things. Express gratitude for what He's doing in your life. Thank Jesus for dying on the cross for you. Thank the Holy Spirit for indwelling you, and never leaving. Thank Him for being your conscience, your counselor and that "still small voice."

Supplication - *"Make your requests known to God."* (Philippians 4:7) Tell God what you want, no matter how small it seems to you. Do you really think any of your requests are big to God the Creator? You should have lots of intercessory prayer here. Remember: As a man of God, you're committed to pray for your pastor and your Church every day.

And if your prayer life becomes stale as 2-week-old bread, change it! If you usually sit in a chair, get on your knees or stand up. Ask God to restore you. Read something. Listen to some music. Sing something. Go to a different place. But don't let it get stale!

Step out in faith and be a Man of Prayer!

Learning to pray is a lot like losing weight, you just have to start. So, today, get on your knees and just pray. Act like you are talking with a buddy about sports, the weather or whatever. Just start talking to God.

Then learn to talk about the most intimate thing in your life—SIN! When you get to a point of sharing your sin with God that is when the power is let loose in your life. Your prayer life will become that of the apostle and not the Pharisees.

Our Challenge to You

After reading this, set some time aside to just talk to God. Let Him know that you just want to talk and share your heat. After you talk, just sit and listen. See if God prompts your heart to make a move, confess a sin or just sit and relax!

CHAPTER NINE

WOMEN OTHER THAN YOUR WIFE

By: Bryan

It doesn't matter what stage of marriage you are currently in, you're going to find yourself around women other than your wife.

QUESTION

Hey man, what am I supposed to do when I find myself attracted to another woman or find a woman other than my wife attracted to me?

ANSWER

You need take a close look at your heart towards your wife and towards God. If they don't have your heart, you won't know what to do with other women.

RELEVANT VERSES

"Do not deprive each other except perhaps by mutual consent and for a time, so that you may devote yourselves to prayer.
Then come together again so that Satan will not tempt you because of your lack of self-control."
-1 Corinthians 7:5

"Therefore put on the full armor of God, so that when the day of evil comes, you may be able to stand your ground, and after you have done everything, to stand."
-Ephesians 6:13

"Marriage should be honored by all,
and the marriage bed kept pure, for God will judge
the adulterer and all the sexually immoral."
-Hebrews 13:4

Personal Testimony

There are a lot of men who start out their marriage and never give a second thought to their relationships with women other than their new wife. I don't think this happens on purpose, I just don't believe the topic is something openly brought up and discussed in today's culture. With that said, most men don't even understand where or how they're going to run into trouble with other women. Well, they're probably looking in the wrong spots. I know I was when I was first married.

The way I see it, there are some very particular areas that can affect a man when it comes to other women. I'm not talking about your family or even close friends; I'm talking about the grey areas, the areas you don't like to admit or even talk about. Here are the three main areas that have affected me and I think you'll be able to relate.

Porn

If your first thought is, *What does porn have to do with other women affecting my marriage?* Then you are in the right chapter. Whether you are just watching on occasion or are totally addicted, you are choosing to put those women on a higher level of importance and intimacy than your wife and even Jesus. I know because it's what I chose to do at the beginning of my marriage.

The college I attended had two things going for me in the wrong directions. The first was it was located hours away from my fiancée. The second was that it was an all guys' campus. What do you get when you put a group of college guys together with limited access to real women or girlfriends? Temptation! Well, temptation and curiosity definitely got the best of me through my years at college. There were a lot of lonely hours and there was really easy access to pornography. The more I did it the more I wanted it.

After three years, it was time to get married. Since no one at the college really cared about my problem and no one at home knew about it, I had a recipe going for an interesting start to marriage. At first, it wasn't too hard. I mean, now that I was married, sex would be readily available, right? Well, even though that was true, I still had the mindset and habit of looking at porn. The real trick became viewing it without my wife knowing it. I knew it wasn't going to last long, but my temptation was stronger than my desire for a strong, healthy marriage. The floor was about to fall out.

In only a matter of moments, in the later hours of one night, my wife woke up early and caught me red-handed. With disbelief and a firestorm of anger, she broke into tears and wondered how I could ever do such a thing to her. I was numb. I was completely unprepared for what to say or how to react, even though I knew I'd get caught eventually. Instead of making Jesus and my wife my desire, I was making the strong addictions of fantasy my desire and I paid for it for many months.

It doesn't matter if you're about to be married, newly married or have been married for many years; pornography will always be a false substitute for the love that Jesus and your wife can provide you.

Past Relationships

Every man has a past and every man deals with his past differently. Past relationships could mean women you went to school with, women you used to date or even women you have divorced. Whatever your history is, you need to make sure none of those women come before your wife. Period!

Some of my personal issues or experiences with past relationships have come from the big social sites. It may be easier to connect than ever to your current friends, but it also includes all of your past friends. This is where I ran into trouble.

I was hanging out on one of the major social sites one night when an old friend, a girl who used to be a friend back in my days before high school, started messaging me. I didn't think anything of it. I assumed she was married now with kids, which seemed obvious from her profile image, and I figured we could catch up. Well, the conversation went on long enough for my wife to notice a conversation going on back and forth. She approached me about my activities and asked what I was doing. I figured it was no big deal, so I told her. Her reaction was quite different than I would have expected. She immediately showed concern about the conversation and asked why I'd be having such a long conversation. At first, I was a little angry at her response, but over time I realized that I was in the wrong. I didn't know this woman anymore and I had no idea of her intentions or current marital situation. I could have been falling into something I'd have no idea how to get out of, similar to my porn story above. I ended up understanding my wife's view of it and have not engaged in that kind of long conversation again unless my wife was involved.

A few years after that, I started noticing some images being posted on a large social site of an old girlfriend of mine. For years I had followed her, and had not really engaged in any conversation. The images started coming in more and more and I knew my wife also followed her. The images were of her and her new fitness career. And I'm not talking about just working out; I'm talking about her becoming a professional body builder. You know, the women who wear the really small swimsuits and show off nearly every part of their body. Whether this was her new hobby or profession, I knew it would only be a matter of time before my wife brought it up to me. Fortunately, I could see the writing on the wall and I un-followed her after only a few images. It was literally the following day that my wife asked me about her and the images. I was honest about seeing the images, but I was also quick to mention that I un-followed her and would not be seeing her anymore.

Even though these are just a couple of small examples, I'm sure they are enough to make you think of some of your own scenarios. Whether it is talking to women online, conversing with particular women at work or even casually hanging out with old friends/ flames; it's important to remember that the relationship with your wife is much more important.

Current Women

Where you find yourself in life now is important to your marriage. It doesn't matter what stage of marriage you are currently in, you are going to find yourself around women other than your wife. Now, this isn't a bad thing and shouldn't be looked at in a negative way, but you should be aware of how these other women could affect your marriage.

Many of us have to talk to other women at the workplace. We have to deal with these women on a daily or weekly basis and it can sometimes be a challenge, especially if you find them attractive or if they dress in a way that distracts you. For others, you know women from the local hang out, Church group or even your neighborhood. You have to recognize and know that other women are going to keep coming up in your life and you need to know how to respect them, but still keep your wife and marriage first.

It's not the first look that will get you hooked; it's the second and third look. I know because that second and third look got the best of me.

The areas I mentioned above are really the early stages of allowing other women into your life and marriage, especially porn. Porn is easily accessible and you already have a past with old relationships, but new women are in a different category. They are fresh and undiscovered. They have an unknown beauty and it can grab a hold of you in an instant if you allow it, especially if you are having trouble in your own marriage or are naive to the effects of other women.

I had gone through the porn stage and had tampered around with old flames when my marriage was going through a tough time. But after getting caught in those areas, as I mentioned above, I naturally moved into the last category and never saw it coming. I slowly started allowing myself to go past the first look and engage in more looks. As the looks continued, they turned into smiles and brief conversations. And as the conversations grew longer, so did my interest in those women. Moving on with that interest will only lead to heartache and divorce. That is exactly where it led me. Because my marriage was failing and because I was allowing other women into my heart, I found myself sitting in a lawyer's office trying to figure out how the process of divorce worked. My heart was in chains that were being pulled in both directions.

Fortunately, God had a bigger plan for me. As I'll soon mention in the chapter on accountability, I was able to speak with a good friend from Church and even my pastor. I was able to share with them the depths of my heart and issues and they were immense help. I was able to recognize the destructive path I was on and I was able to close the doors on all of those other interests. In short, I closed the door to other women and re-opened the door to Jesus. It was the best move I ever made in my life and for my marriage.

Take a few moments this week and assess your current relationships with women other than your wife. Are you doing things for one woman that you're not doing for your wife? Are you keeping those around you aware that you are happily married? Are you affirming your love to your wife each day? Consider these next sections and take the necessary actions!

Here are four main issues I had when it came to other women.

I forgot the importance of my vows.

I thought that looking at other women wasn't a big deal.

My wife and I didn't discuss how to deal with the opposite sex early in our marriage.

I allowed disputes and misunderstandings with my wife to go unresolved.

Here are four areas I now recognize about myself.

I recognize distraction and temptation when I first see it. Once I process it, I turn away from it and seek help in prayer.

I recognize my areas of weakness. Once I feel that pull towards another woman, I understand why and seek strength in Christ.

I recognize that my relationship with my wife can affect my relationship with other women. Once I find myself distracted, I need to go back and make sure the relationship with my wife is good. If not, seek prayer and resolution with her.

I recognize that false desires and temptation will not only affect my marriage, but will also affect my relationship with Christ. I know that if I keep those relationships first in my life, they will give me strength when I do catch that first look.

Here are 5 things you can do to improve your relationship with your wife and keep healthy relationships with women other than your wife.

1) Talk to your wife early, or now, about relationships with the opposite sex and establish some ground rules.

2) Go back to your vows and really understand their meaning and depth. Then strive to live up to them daily.

3) Keep a healthy and intimate relationship with your wife. Go out on a monthly date and talk about issue of the heart. Don't be afraid to help each other.

4) Be honest with your wife when you do have to encounter another woman or if you had a brief encounter with another woman.

5) Pray for your wife and marriage daily. This is where you'll make the biggest positive impact in your marriage.

Our Challenge to You

Take a few moments now and consider all of your relationships with other women. Pray for those relationships and make sure they are honoring your God and your wife.

Have you ever discussed the relationships you have with the opposite sex, with your wife? Prayerfully consider this idea today and recognize it as a positive strength for your marriage.

Taking a hard look at these issues will make a huge, positive impact in your marriage. Don't deny these areas of struggle or potential struggle any longer. Take action today

CHAPTER TEN

BEING SMART ABOUT BEING ONLINE

By: Bryan

Don't ever assume that the ice you're standing on is thick enough to hold you.

QUESTION

Hey man, what are some ways my wife and I can protect our marriage and ourselves while we are online or on social media?

ANSWER

You need to be completely honest about your actions & allow each other access to anything.

RELEVANT VERSES

"Create in me a pure heart, O God,
and renew a steadfast spirit within me."
-Psalm 51:10

"Your enemy the devil prowls around like a roaring lion looking for someone to devour. Resist him, standing firm in the faith, because you know that the family of believers throughout the world is undergoing the same kind of sufferings."
-1 Peter 5:8-9

"Like a city whose walls are broken througH
is a person who lacks self-control."
-Proverbs 25:28

My Personal Battle and Getting Caught

Has your wife ever come up to you randomly and asked if she could borrow your phone? For some of you your heart probably dropped to the floor and fear slapped you in the face. For others it may not be a big deal. I suppose it all depends on what you are up to. I can honestly say that I had a fear of her asking no matter what device she asked me to use.

It didn't matter if I was on the computer or my phone, if I was alone, I was tempted to go to sites and look at things I knew were wrong. And after enough debate with a relentless enemy, I would often give in. And once I gave in and then got out of it, it was a fight against the clock to erase my actions and make sure my wife couldn't figure out what I was up to. Don't ever assume that the ice you're standing on is thick enough to hold you.

I spoke of my personal example more in the chapter entitled "Other Women"; there was that time where my wife caught me off guard and she saw everything that I had been viewing online. Whatever string was holding up our relationship was now severed and we crumbled quickly; all because I couldn't keep my eyes and heart focused on God and my wife. These are some of my biggest regrets from earlier in my marriage.

Don't live in a way that your wife can't go on any device and know that you are being an honest and mature husband. It's not, and never will be, worth it.

Being Smart When You Are Being Social

Just type in "social media and marriage" and you'll find that over 32% of marriages are more likely to end in divorce when they heavily use social media. That may be a painful statistic, but I can see how easily it can happen.

I have had the fortunate and unfortunate blessing of growing up during the most intense tech boom in history. I can still remember setting up my first online social account and becoming friends with people I knew and didn't know. At the time, it was just exciting to be online and have people follow me. Even though they were strangers, I still felt important and glad that people wanted to know me.

What came next changed everything though. We now live in a time where over a billion people are on social media sites. Family who you might have never met or hardly see can now track your every move. Friends who you thought you escaped at graduation are now sending you "friend requests", and you're left with a decision to accept or not. And, of course, women you use to date or thought were good looking in the past are now just a click away.

Here are 10 things to help you have a safer and better experience while you are online or using social media.

1) Protect Yourself against Temptation

Finding ways to protect yourself while you are online or on your social media timeline is critical to staying consistent and honest with your wife; you simply can't assume you have it all under control, especially if you have struggled with particular issues in the past. Take the time to set up safeguards. For more on this topic, I encourage you to re-read the chapter by Jody on pornography.

2) Keep the Computer/Tablets in the Main Rooms

A few years ago, a couple from Church invited us over to their house for a get-together. There were other young and married couples there and it was set to be a great time. Being that this was the first time we were at their house, I noticed something interesting. The family computer wasn't in an office or even in a back room somewhere; it was located just off the side of the living room. I thought this was odd, considering our main computer was located in our small office, but never asked my friend about it that night.

As our friendship grew over the next few years, we finally had a conversation about his computer and the reasons for its location. He said it was put there so that there was minimal temptation to look at things he shouldn't or talk to people he shouldn't. He knew that his wife or even one of his daughters could walk in at any moment and that was enough for him not to make any wrong or painful moves. I really respected his view and appreciated his honesty.

Where is your home computer located? Could it be moved to a better, more conspicuous location in your home? The same could go for your tablet or laptop usage. Instead of escaping into the man cave or the back office, you could make an effort to use it only in the living room or another open location. As I am typing this now, I am sitting in my kitchen and I know that my wife could arrive home at any moment.

Take some time to consider the locations of your computers and ask yourself if you need to make some changes. Take the initiative to make the necessary moves to safeguard your marriage.

3) Have a Plan for When Distraction Takes Over

Just as I mentioned at the beginning of this chapter, it is important to have a plan for when you suddenly find yourself alone and distracted with temptations.

"Alright honey, I'll be back in a couple of hours!" This is what my wife has said to me many times and 9 times out of 10 my first thoughts are about temptations. My first battle right after she closes the door is not to look at things I shouldn't and engage in activities that I know hurt the intimacy with my wife. But how do you fight off the temptation?

Just as Jody spoke about programs and accountability in the first point and in his chapter, I'll add that having a plan in place is essential to beating distractions. Here are a few of the options I keep in mind. The first thing I do is pray. I discuss the temptations with God and go to battle with Him over the necessity of them. From there, I run through a brief list of other options. I could go for a run. I could clean the house. I could turn on some music to help my mind stay focused on other things. I could also leave and just go for a drive or visit the local hardware store. Doing something is better than falling.

When my wife and I were in the midst of rebuilding our marriage, I wanted more than anything to keep my word and promises to her. There were some days when I'd get out of work early and, instead of leaving right away, I found myself just sitting in my car. At the time, I really enjoyed a racing app on my phone, so I just sat back and played it. When the time came that I could go home and my wife would be there, I'd finish up and leave. Just that little bit of discipline saved me a lot of heartache and pain.

What is your plan for when distractions take over? Do you have one? Have you ever even considered needing one? Take some time to review these questions and take action on them today.

4) Allow Your Wife to View Any Device at Any Time

Imagine how good it would feel if you knew there was no reason for your wife to be concerned about your online activities. Imagine how freeing it would be if she could ask for your phone or get on your computer at any point and know that you have not been looking at or doing things you shouldn't on these devices. Those feelings of relief, comfort and trust are exactly where you want your marriage to be at on a consistent basis.

My challenge for you is to be and feel completely free in this area. I can assure you that, when you make the attempt to be honest about your activity or allow your wife to view your activities, there will be an enemy working against you. He will show you options to get around this, such as deleting your history or accessing inappropriate material through apps. It's critical to dismiss these thoughts and ideas as soon as they enter your head. Your main goal is not to hide what you are doing from your wife; rather it is to be honest about what you are doing with your wife. Don't let a very active enemy try to fool you otherwise. His attacks will be strong, but you must fight back in the name of Jesus!

Consider your recent actions online and ask yourself if you can be trusted. Could your wife go on any device of yours and be free to look anywhere she wanted? What would it mean to your wife and marriage if you could allow this process to happen and for it to go smoothly every time?

5) Un-friend Those Who Post Inappropriate Images/Material

Not too long ago, I was sitting next to my wife on our couch. It had been a long day between our son and our work, so she was playing her games and I was checking out one of my social accounts. As I scrolled through my timeline, there appeared a half-naked woman on the screen. I could have sworn the woman in the image was suddenly in person and in the room. I immediately reacted to the image and continued scrolling. Fortunately, my wife was busy on her phone and didn't see the image.

This is something I don't want to happen in my marriage. Especially given the circumstances I shared from the chapter "Other Women". What I did next is something I suggest you consider as you move forward; I removed the person who posted the image from my friends list. Does it matter who is posting the material? Well, in this circumstance it was a cousin of mine who I hardly see and I had no problem cutting ties with him online. My wife and my marriage are worth leaps and bounds more than his personal desires.

Another reason to un-friend those who post inappropriate things is because of your past. Have you had a hard time looking at porn in the past? Do you stumble easily when you are faced with those images? If so, the last thing you need is to follow someone who posts them on your timeline. Again, your marriage and your wife are worth more than that.

Take a moment today and consider those you follow on social media. Is there anyone you need to confront? Is there anyone you need to un-follow for the greater good of your marriage? Take necessary action today!

6) Never Defend Someone Online against Your Wife

"He probably posted those inappropriate images online because he is lonely. I'll let him know he needs to stop." "He just posted the image as a joke. Don't get so worked up."

Have you ever found yourself saying something like the above quotes to your wife? If so, this can be one of the worst moves you make. It's reminds me of similar times when my wife and I are in large groups of friends or family and I do or say something that is wildly inappropriate about her. These are not the ways to treat your wife online or in real life.

If you find yourself defending someone else's behavior or actions, you need to take a step back. You need to recognize that your wife is now the most important relationship in your life and the person you're defending is more than likely an old friend who no longer plays a vital part in your life anymore. In other words, it's time to move on. It's time to Man Up and focus on your wife and your marriage. Support and defend her whenever you can!

Take some time to think about your past behavior. Have there been times when you've defended an old friend rather than your wife? If so, seek forgiveness from your wife quickly and let her know your status on things moving forward. She will appreciate the support.

7) Don't Get Involved with Women of Previous Interest or Relationship

To be completely honest with you, there are probably 5-10 women I either used to know or took an interest in at one point in my life or another on my social media requests page who I have refused to be friends with. Their requests don't go un-noticed, but I can't think of any good reasons to be friends with them online— pictures of their vacations with their spouses or boyfriends or, worse yet, images of them doing things I have no business knowing about. My marriage is more important.

Some of the guys who might have the hardest time with this concept are the ones who recently married. There's a good chance that both you and your wife have friends of the opposite sex. This isn't the time to assume that nothing bad could happen or be surprised when something does happen to come up. Set aside some time early in your marriage to discuss friendships with the opposite sex and set some ground rules. Set some rules for when you actually meet up with people and how you can interact with them online.

Take some time this week to review your relationships with other women online. Are you following someone you know you shouldn't? Are you following someone and if your wife knew she would disagree with it? Answer these questions and take action!

8) Only Share Positive Updates and Images

As the years have passed and I have become more mature in my marriage and online activities, I now only post things of a positive nature. I love to share great photos of my beautiful wife and myself together. I enjoy sharing funny photos of my three-year-old son doing awesome and sometimes ridiculous things. All of these images along with an occasional positive update about my life or marriage are a great way to show others that your marriage is strong and ongoing.

One of the worst moves you can make is to share negative personal feelings online either with people you know or people who might sympathize with you on a random website. There are people out there who love to see that there are things wrong with your life. There are those out there who don't have any desire to help you, but will only lead you down a worse path. If you need help in your marriage or if you need some advice, try to seek out good men from your Church or even your pastor. Keep private things private.

What have you been posting online lately? Have you been searching for affirmation or for answers in places or websites you know you shouldn't? Make it a goal to only post positive things and images about your life, family and marriage.

9) Don't Get Involved with Social Media at All

My wife and I sometimes feel like we fall into the gap where we know a ton about technology, and friends who are just a few years older know nearly nothing about technology or social media. I'm not sure if I envy them or question them.

What does set them apart, far apart, from the majority these days is their choice not to engage in anything to do with social media. They have never had a social media account and they don't have smartphones. Yes, they know about all of the options but they have chosen to keep their distance from them. They see them more as distractions from each other and can't find the need to add them to their already busy lives. I can't blame them.

I've talked to my buddy about this on multiple occasions and yet he never gives into my pressure or the pressure from anyone else. He works with men of all different ages and gets to hear enough drama from men who are looking at things they shouldn't or talking about getting involved with the wrong women online. Since he has a strong marriage, he can offer advice on the deeper issue and doesn't even need to address the online behavior.

Take some time to consider this one question; would it benefit my marriage more or less if I gave up my activities on a particular social network? Take your time with this one and discuss options with your wife as well.

10) Schedule Time Away from Your Tech and Social Media

It was just the other weekend that my wife and I were out finishing up some shopping before the holidays. Since it was getting late in the day, we decided to find a nice restaurant for some dinner. Once seated, we noticed another couple sitting beside us. They weren't talking to each other; they were both on their phones. This didn't go on for just a moment; they stayed on their phones until their food came. My wife and I figured it might have been a blind date that wasn't going so well. When they went to leave the restaurant before us, we noticed that she was pregnant! This wasn't a new couple at all; this was a very established couple that had hardly any communication skills. It was also a good reminder for our own marriage.

Our Challenge to You

A lot of ground was covered in this chapter, but it was all important. If social media issues keep coming up in your marriage, I encourage you to review the 10 items listed above. Highlight which ones are affecting your marriage and take action on them this week. You have the tools, now it's up to you to get things done.

CHAPTER ELEVEN

MANAGE EXPECTATIONS

By: Jody

Once you have decided on the expectation for each of you, stick to it!

QUESTION

What are false expectations and how do they affect my marriage?

ANSWER

A-S-S-U-M-E (I'm sure you know what this stands for).

RELEVANT VERSE

"...until we all reach unity in the faith and in the knowledge of the Son of God and become mature, attaining to the whole measure of the fullness of Christ."
-Ephesians 4:13

The Problem

Many times in a marriage there is very little communication. Studies show that this tends to be a big reason for fights and, unfortunately, divorce. A couple falls in "lust", not love; they then get married and, when things get hard, they quit trying or become complacent and things start to fall apart. Communication pretty much comes to a halt.

When we start assuming we know what is best for us and our spouse, we set ourselves up for failure. Unrealistic expectations take over because of our "assumed" thoughts or actions; we begin to create a marriage that becomes a relationship based on false expectations. Let me give you an example:

You get off work! It's been a hard day and you feel like you just want to sit on the couch. You have used up all your words and all you can do is grunt. It's been that kind of day.

But your wife has a different plan! She needs you to help with the dinner because, due to a sick kid and the oldest kid having soccer practice, she is running late.

Now, one of two things can happen here. First, she gets mad because you tell her no and sit on the couch anyway. In your words, "I'm just too tired." Or, second, you get mad because in your mind you say, *I have to do everything in this house.*

Consider how we talk about sex. If you're a man and have two eyes and two balls, you tend to want to have sex daily. So when you try to make a move on our wife, she says, "No," or maybe she says, "You want it all the time," or, "You're never satisfied," and this makes us frustrated! Again, this is something that has never been communicated to her.

Personal Testimony

In 2011, my wife and I had our first child, a beautiful baby girl. We had been married 12 years before this day so we had a lot of our own routine down. My wife did her thing and I did mine and we would meet in the middle most of the time.

After we brought our little girl home from the hospital, I hired a full-time nanny so my wife could go back to work and we could get back to creating our kingdom. This is what we did for 12 years, so that is what we were going to continue to do.

About 18 months later, we had a beautiful baby boy. A few weeks later, he was with the full-time nanny, as our daughter was, and we were back to building our kingdom. And I was happy and so was my wife, or so I thought.

For most of my adult life, I have been focused on making money, period! I didn't think about family in the process just the money. I assumed my wife liked it as much as I did but that wasn't the case. She was starting to see that being an adult was a lot more than making money. It involved adult things like raising a family and not letting some other woman do it. I had blinders on.

So, naturally, when I didn't get the drift that my wife was miserable, she let me have it. My lack of caring about her feelings led me to believe expectations that weren't real. She didn't care about the money like I did and I didn't care about the kids like she did. So we were on opposite ends of the spectrum.

It wasn't until she threw a fit that I actually got the point of her misery. I wasn't being the father or husband I needed to be and she couldn't be the mother she wanted to be because she had to work. This caused major problems in our marriage until we understood each other's expectations.

The Solution

Ever been there—assuming your wife is thinking or feeling the same thing you are then coming to find out you're not even on the same planet together? It's frustrating and can make you feel helpless. I've been there and it's no fun!

So, let me give you five things you can do to help you with realistic expectations.

Communicate

This should be obvious but, in reality, it is the hardest thing for us to do! Learn to talk out situations and expectations of your marriage. Find out what your wife wants and let her know what you want. It shouldn't matter what the topic is, talk about it! Sex, money, kids, cleaning the house, working late, etc. Make sure you know what to expect and what she expects.

Stick to it

Once you have decided on the expectation for each of you, stick to it! Be sure to keep your side of the bargain! If she has an expectation of you spending time with the kids once or twice a week, do it. If she needs you to clean the house on the weekend or come home and cook dinner, do it. Every now and then, revisit your expectations just to make sure you are both meeting them.

Make a schedule

This might seem weird at first, but with our busy lives this makes a lot of sense. Schedule your expectations. Let's say she wants you to help clean the house. Put it on the schedule. Say every Tuesday night is house cleaning. How about a date night? Every other Friday night, you are going to put a date night on the schedule. Just get it on the calendar then stick to it.

Read the Word together

Of all the things that will help you become unified, reading your Bible together will be the most profitable thing you can do for your marriage. Start off with once or twice a week. Just sit down and pick out a passage, a chapter or a book and start reading. Then sit and discuss what you two think God is saying. It's a great conversation starter.

Pray together

This is something we all need more of, prayer! As a couple, this needs to be a priority. Learn to sit quietly and pray with each other. This should be a daily ritual.

Our Challenge to You

After reading this, set some time aside with your spouse. Let her know that you would like to open up a conversation in order to help each other meet each other's expectations. Don't just walk into the other room and spring it on her, give her a time and date and schedule it. Then give her the topics you would like to discuss and let her get her thoughts in order as well.

CHAPTER TWELVE

ESTABLISH YOUR PRIORITIES

By: Bryan

A mature husband doesn't simply hope;
he plans!

Your most important relationship began
when you met your wife, it got even
stronger when you married her!

QUESTION

How comes things won't change in my marriage?

ANSWER

Things won't change in your marriage until you review and establish your priorities!

RELEVANT VERSES

"Flee the evil desires of youth and pursue righteousness, faith, love and peace, along with those who call on the Lord out of a pure heart."
-2 Timothy 2:22

"For where your treasure is, there your heart will be also."
-Luke 12:34

Adjust Your Priorities

As I've mentioned in other chapters, my wife and I struggled hard in our early years of marriage. We knew we needed to find and establish ourselves at a good home church, but we put it off for our first few years.

I'd wake up, every Sunday morning, thinking about church. I'd lie there in bed staring at the ceiling wanting to ask her to go, but I always held back. There was a war going on in my head of wishing I could do what was needed and right, but never bringing myself to do it.

On one Sunday morning in particular, we slept in long enough to where we knew going to church was no longer an option. Instead of talking about it, we decided to get some lunch at a bar type restaurant near our house. We were some of the few that were actually there that early on a Sunday morning. We immediately felt out of place, but we went with it. We ate the greasy bar food and then proceeded to play some pool. The music was loud and obnoxious; it had an extra essence to it that just made you feel even dirtier than you already felt. We missed out on the blessings of church with this garbage. It was time for a change.

Although I felt awful that I took my wife to such a place on a Sunday morning, it was through this experience that I realized I needed to adjust my priorities. It was after this that we started talking about church and why we were not going. From there on out, I fought the fear of asking and started asking her every Saturday night about church. We weren't going to wonder about it anymore or wait till the last second, we decided to make it a priority and go to church on Sunday mornings.

A mature husband doesn't simply hope; he plans!

Through that experience, God taught me a lot about leadership in my marriage. He taught me that a husband must learn to prioritize, or the enemy will attempt to prioritize my life for me. Every husband must learn that the vows he spoke to his wife, and in front of God and his family, meant change was required!

Here are some simple questions I want you to review and answer. As with other challenges laid out in this book, you can simply review them in your head or you can step it up and write down each question and answer. Take this seriously guys!

"Am I making my marriage a priority?"

"Are the vows I spoke to my wife changing my priorities?"

"Is my wife a priority?"

Don't be fooled! Although these questions might sound basic, they are far from it!

Your marriage requires a serious change in priorities. These changes could happen with your work, with your friends and with your overall time management. I want to take each of these areas and break them down with you.

Work

Work is essential in providing for your marriage. It offers your marriage security, safety and peace of mind financially. What work should not be, is more important than your relationship with your wife. It should not always be getting you up early and out late. It's needed for support, but it's not meant to dominate.

I work in commercial construction, so I know how easy it is to work long hours, especially if my wife and I are not getting along. There have been times when I'd intentionally get up an hour or two early, not to spend time with God or anything, just as a way to get out of the house. A way to not have to engage in another heated discussion over something stupid. On the opposite spectrum, I use to get out of work around 4, but not make it home until 7 or 8. Or I'd just work till 7 or 8. I was living in fear of having a real and deep conversation with my wife. I was being a coward.

As the years have passed and our marriage has improved, there are still those times that work requires my extra time, but now I plan for it. This always occurs when projects are ending and my co-workers and I are trying to complete a building. On recent projects that were ending, I've taken my wife out for a nice dinner in advance of the crazy hours; a time where we can just be with each other and have real conversations. I use this time to give her the warning or the heads up that work is going to require more of my attention during the coming weeks or even weekends. She has become use to this idea, but also hopes that when I am home or when these extra hours end, that my attention goes back to her the way it should be. This process of giving her notice before, then giving her needed attention afterwards has really improved our relationship.

Just a little bit of planning with your wife will show her that she is still and always will be your top priority!

I want you to take a moment and assess your current workload. Does it allow a way to not just provide, but also make your marriage a priority? Would adjusting your hours, moving to a new job or position allow you more quality time with your wife? If action is needed in this area, step up and start making changes now.

Friends

Friends are absolutely necessary, especially in terms of accountability, which we will discuss in the next chapter. But your friends should not be getting more quality time than your wife is getting, deserves and needs. Your most important relationship began when you met your wife, and it got even stronger when you married her!

One of the biggest mistakes men make when it comes to friends, is their relationship with other women. I know we've discussed other women in other chapters, but what about the ones your friends with before you were married? You must consider how that relationship has to change after speaking your vows. It is critical that you discuss those existing relationships with your wife to get her feel on it. She now has a huge say in that area.

Another way your marriage will struggle is spending excessive amounts of time out with your buddies. Meeting at the bar, playing basketball at the gym every day or engaging in a time consuming hobby. I'm not saying to not do these things, but I am saying you must be respectful of your wife's needs as well. Especially if her love language is quality time! I believe this goes back to my planning statement above. A mature husband will establish a balance and will plan accordingly. Again, make spending time with your wife a priority!

Along with work, I challenge you to take some time to review your current friendships. Is that old friend pulling you away from your new marriage? Are your friends getting more of your quality self than your wife is? Answer these questions and make the necessary adjustments!

Time Management

Time management is something you have to practice and maintain for your work. Arrive on time or early and leave when it's appropriate and not too early. We practice time management in our hobbies, sports and guy time's right?

You don't miss a tee time.

You don't miss the kickoff.

You don't miss the drop of the green flag.

You prioritize what is important to you!

But the real challenge is your own marriage. That's important to you right? It's essential to practice time management in your marriage. If you work all day Friday, then go out with the guys Friday night, then tee off at 7am the next morning; what about your wife?

Where does she fit into all of this timing? Better yet, when does she get what's left of you?

What's left of you? Let that last line sink in for a moment. Your wife doesn't deserve what's left of you; she deserves the best of you!

Personally, I've always struggled with time management in my marriage. My wife would tell me about something coming up; I'd nod in agreement and then totally miss it. Why, because I was likely on the phone or watching the race. She didn't get my full attention and I didn't make her scheduling statement a priority. Guys, it's in our best interest to set down the phone or pause the TV while your wife is planning with you. Don't get frustrated that she's "interrupting" your "important" time, give her the attention she needs for those few moments and then make note of it! Over the last few years I've started to improve in this area by harnessing the power of the technology that's with most of us every day, our phones. As soon as something important is mentioned or a date is set, mark it down in your phone calendar and add early reminders. Just a few seconds of your time will help improve your marriage and show your wife that her needs are top priority!

Along with work and friendships, take some time to assess your time management. Who is getting all of your time, your quality time? Is it actually your wife?

Learn to make your marriage a priority and it will thrive!

Our Challenge to You

We challenge you to closely review each of these three areas in your own life. Take a few moments now to pray about each topic. Decide which one needs the most work first. Define a plan for real change and start taking action. If more than one area requires considerable work, don't panic, take each one in strides and real change will come to you and your marriage.

CHAPTER THIRTEEN

THE IMPORTANCE OF ACCOUNTABILITY

By: Bryan

One of the first things my wife and I should have done after our wedding was found a good home Church.

Iron sharpens iron isn't a verse about iron, it's about the critical role other men play in the lives of other men.

QUESTION

Hey man, should I be telling my wife every time
I sin or feel tempted towards another woman?

ANSWER

You should always be honest with your wife,
but you need a male accountability partner
to discuss these hard issues with as well.

RELEVANT VERSES

"And let us consider how we may spur one another on
toward love and good deeds, not giving up meeting
together, as some are in the habit of doing, but
encouraging one another—and all the more
as you see the Day approaching."
-Hebrews 10:24-25

"As iron sharpens iron,
so one person sharpens another."
-Proverbs 27:17

"Therefore put on the full armor of God, so that when
the day of evil comes, you may be able to stand your
ground, and after you have done everything, to stand."
-Ephesians 6:13

My Personal Testimony

Before my wife and I got married, and even for a year or so after the wedding, I thought she would be the only person I would ever need. We had dated for nearly 6 years and we thought marriage would be easy and wonderful. Time would eventually prove me wrong.

As the second year approached, our relationship had started to deteriorate rapidly. We found ourselves having more and more disagreements, and it eventually turned into weekly yelling matches. And although those matches felt good to my self-righteous heart, they were getting us absolutely nowhere. Well, I say nowhere, but they were actually leading us straight towards divorce. I never thought I'd see the day, but I didn't know what else to do.

As I reflect back now on thinking "I didn't know what else to do," I realize how absent-minded I really was at the time. I realized the fog that the enemy had us in and can't believe he was able to convince us of so much. So much that I thought divorce or another woman must have been the answer.

The truth is I was blind to the most obvious ways to get help for myself and for my marriage.

Looking back, here are the three ways I should have been looking for help.

Jesus

I'll be completely honest with you, even though I grew up in a Christian home and always attended a Christian school; I had no idea how important a relationship with Jesus would be in my life. Jesus always came across as more of a set of rules than a relationship to be had. And since I had never been married, I never thought He'd make any impact in my marriage. I wasn't just wrong, I was really wrong.

One of the first things my wife and I should have done after our wedding was found a good home Church. I honestly should have taken a better and stronger lead with this process. Instead, we would wake up on Sunday morning and wonder if the other person would mention Church or not. If it wasn't mentioned then neither of us would push the issue, even though it was in the back of both of our minds. This, of course, was the attitude we took towards Church and Jesus during those rough early years of marriage. It's pretty obvious to see why we struggled so badly.

Jesus proved to be an accountability partner that I didn't want to confront in those early years. As I said, I thought my wife and I would be enough for each other. What could Jesus offer? Why should we spend our time learning about Him? Those simple, yet very important, questions were finally answered and realized as my wife and I approached our third year of marriage. We were both able to recognize the need for Him in both of our lives as individuals and in our marriage. He must be at the center of your marriage.

Jesus is now my number one accountability partner. Instead of turning to alcohol, the local hangout or even just avoiding my issues, I turn to Him. He's readily available and waiting for you.

My Pastor

My wife and I did finally find a Church to attend during our harder earlier years, but it still wasn't treated as a critical activity. Attendance was still optional and occasional to say the least. We didn't even attend the regular service very often; we attended a marriage class once in a while, probably more out of guilt than necessity.

But even with that lazy mindset, we still put ourselves in front of a better crowd and a better influence of people. Most of the other couples in the class had already been through hard times and were there to learn more about their marriage or help other couples. We needed help.

Through those classes, it was good to learn and realize that other couples were going through similar issues. It was good to know that not all other marriages were perfect. The classes allowed me to open up more about particular marriage issues, but I never felt like I could really let it all out. I never felt completely free and open to share the deeper parts of my heart.

Our pastor was older than me, but younger than most pastors. After speaking with him a few times in general and hearing some of his sermons, I felt like I could really relate to him. He understood the troubles in marriage. He experienced the issues of lust and temptation. He was still human, right? And in my search for answers and help, I finally decided to set up a meeting with him. I'm glad to this day that I did.

Meeting with my pastor turned out to be one of the best accountability times I had ever experienced up to that point in my life. He could laugh and relate to almost all of my stories and complaints, but offered sound advice on what I was doing wrong. It was exactly what I needed to hear. I was able to be more open with him than I had been with the groups. He would ask me hard questions that no one had asked me before. And at the end, he challenged me to read the scriptures more and to find out what it meant to be a Christian on my own terms. For too long, I had listened to what everyone else was saying and just gone with it. It was time to take responsibility. It was shortly after this experience that God led me to start my site, Manturity.com.

My pastor and I are now closer because of my willingness to be open and honest. He knows the deeper issues of my heart and he still accepts me. His role as pastor is important to me, but his role as accountability partner is critical.

Other Men

Iron sharpens iron isn't a verse about iron, it's about the critical role other men play in the lives of other men. Without the more experienced iron giving me some hard and honest challenges, I might not have become the man I am today. I might not even be married.

As I mentioned in earlier paragraphs, joining a small group class helped me relate to other men. And it was through some of those men that I was able to get past the darts of the enemy and be the man I am today. Even though I thought I could make it on my own or I thought that my wife would be enough, God knew the truth and He had a plan for me. He lined up men to show up in my life at the right time.

I avoided the first few attempts at meeting another guy from Church to discuss my marriage. What could he offer? How could he have any idea what I was going through? I was selfish and immature. When I finally did agree to meet with him, I tried to be cool. I attempted to play off my issues as not that big of a deal and stay away from the problems of my heart. Well, my buddy could see right through me and I'm glad he could.

He shared stories, crazy stories, about the times in his marriage when he felt like divorce was the absolute best answer. Some of his stories even made some of my situations look like nothing. They didn't even sound real, especially since his marriage was so good right then. I did the right thing though, and shut my mouth and listened to what he had to say. I asked him various questions about his stories and how he managed to survive. He was open and willing to talk about all of it. And, finally, he shared how he made it through and how his marriage was still tough at times, but better than ever before. I wanted to know more.

And more is exactly what he told me. I learned through meeting with my buddy from Church that no marriage is perfect but there is a lot more to it than first thought. He made me realize that, although my marriage issues were bad, there was always hope for forgiveness and resolution. We have been friends ever since and I still turn to him during hard or confusing times.

Having a brother as an accountability partner is one of the strongest moves a man can make. You can both provide support when needed and never feel alone. There's a brother out there who needs you and you need him—so get out there and open up.

Our Challenge to You

When is the last time you called a brother who you knew needed help? When was the last time you honestly opened up to someone about your deepest struggles?

Accountability can be the difference between saving your marriage and ending it. It can be the difference between finding another woman to confide in and staying true to your wife. You need to have someone holding you accountable.

So what are you going to do about it?

Here are 5 ways to get started with accountability this week:

PRAY

Take some time to pray this week. Pray that God will show you the areas in your life that you need to get honest about. Pray that God will provide you with ways and opportunities to meet other men. Pray that God will give you the courage to be consistent with whomever God puts you with.

REACH OUT

Keep your heart open to who would make a good accountability partner. Pray with your main partner, Jesus. Reach out to your pastor and ask him for his thoughts on who to connect with. And, finally, if you know some men already, set aside your pride and ask them to help you out. Trust me; they need it too.

SET A TIME AND PLACE

Once you've reached out and established a partner or two, set up a time and a place to meet. This doesn't need to be fancy; try to meet up at a local restaurant or even a small café. Try to use the time to discuss deeper matters of the heart rather than the latest sports games. And before you leave, set up the next time and place to meet again.

PICK A TOPIC

After you start meeting regularly and start getting to know your partners, start to pick certain topics to discuss. What are you struggling with? What do you want to learn more about? Learn and answer questions together and make a real impact in your walk with Christ.

BE CONSISTENT

I always say that it's hard to start something but it's even harder to maintain something. Your time with your accountability partners needs to be treated as a critical life activity. Time with Jesus can be set for every day, times with your pastor can be set as needed and times with brothers should be weekly or no less than monthly. Be intentional and consistent!

CHAPTER FOURTEEN

EVERY MARRIAGE NEEDS A MAINTENANCE PLAN

By: Bryan

If you take the time to walk with Christ while you are on your own and while you are away from your wife, you will always come back to her a stronger man.

Real marriage maintenance requires real consistency.

QUESTION

Hey man, there are times when I feel really
close to my wife and Jesus,
but then it seems to fade.
How can I be more consistent?

ANSWER

You need to build a real battle plan for yourself
and for your marriage that establishes
maintenance goals each year of your marriage.

RELEVANT VERSES

"Fight the good fight of faith."
-1 Timothy 6:12

"Then we will no longer be infants, tossed back and
forth by the waves, and blown here and there by every
wind of teaching and by the cunning and craftiness of
people in their deceitful scheming. Instead, speaking
the truth in love, we will grow to become in every
respect the mature body of him who
is the head, that is, Christ."
-Ephesians 4:14-15

"But we also glory in our sufferings, because we know
that suffering produces perseverance; perseverance,
character; and character, hope."
-Romans 5:3-4

What Is Maintenance?

In order for a man to find the value in maintaining his marriage, he needs to first understand what maintenance is and what it is not. Maintenance is preservation. When you own a car there is a list of maintenance items you are required to perform on it in order to preserve it. This isn't magical news to anyone, but it's an important parallel to understanding your marriage. Maintenance is also an effort to keep things in an appropriate condition. When I'm cruising along the highway at 70, I don't take any notice of the nice, smooth road I am driving on but when the road has consistent bumps, repairs, holes and more it becomes the only thing I notice. The road in bad condition has not been kept in an appropriate condition. It has been neglected and therefore it is in rough shape. The same will become true of your marriage if it is not maintained and kept in an appropriate condition. The bumps and bruises along the way will become the only thing you notice and your marriage will quickly backslide.

The idea of maintaining your marriage and the word assumption should never be in the same category. But, unfortunately for many couples, they think that the wedding day is the end of the learning curve for them. They blindly believe and assume that everything will now just suddenly work out. Trust will suddenly no longer be a concern to either of them. I mean they said their vows, right? Many couples will assume that they can just figure it out on their own. Being in love and being married does not produce a perfect Garden of Eden experience where you suddenly know everything there is to know about your spouse. In fact, it is the complete opposite. The day you said your vows was the beginning of your journey into the unknown. That is why it is so critical to have your relationship with Jesus right and have an established battle plan. Every man needs a mentor and a guide going into the marriage unknown, which is why we have Jesus ready and available to help us. Marriage will be tough at times and you should never assume anything, but instead take all your needs to Jesus. Ask Him how you can better maintain your marriage from day one!

My Personal Journey

Performing maintenance in my marriage took some time to get right. I am reminded of a time when I went to buy a used vehicle a few years ago. It was a Ford F-150 and it was super clean. I arrived at the seller's house and gave it a good review. It was very clean on the outside with no rust and hardly any dents. The interior was pretty clean as well. The seats weren't worn out and the plastic wasn't beat up and scratched. I really thought this was the one. But then I asked him about the service records. He didn't have any, not one. I proceeded to pop the hood and review the engine. I could tell it was going to need some work. I then checked the oil and it didn't even register on the dipstick. I asked him when the oil had last been changed and he struggled to put a date on it. Even though the truck looked super clean overall, there was a good chance it didn't have much more running life in it. I had to turn it down.

It's easy to put on the nice clothes, shake a few hands and smile at those around you; but it means nothing if your marriage is dead once you leave those around you.

It took about three years for my wife and me to realize we needed to be more intentional in maintaining our marriage. We needed to stop assuming we knew everything and start actually learning what God had originally intended our marriage to be like. We finally started to attend a small group at our Church. This group was with other married couples that were, for the most part, our age. We would watch a DVD lesson that would last about 30 minutes and then discuss the main topics for about another hour. These classes were great for three reasons. The first was that we realized we were not alone when it came to our issues. The second was that we were able to make some great friends from the classes. The third was that we were learning how to improve our marriage. We were taking the time to learn about it, maintain it and make it better. We figured that, even if we only got one good tip from the entire class, it would be worth it!

How to Approach Maintenance

Maintenance wasn't something my wife and I talked about before marriage. It wasn't even brought up in our pre-marriage counseling. Our focus at the time was getting married, getting jobs and moving to a new state. Yes, we were crazy, but we were also in our early twenties and completely clueless.

We spent the next couple of years making bigger and bigger potholes in our road of marriage. It was a terrible road to drive on every day and we didn't know what to do. The worst part about it was that we were unwilling to seek help. As badly as we were doing, we didn't want to let anyone else know. We were the shiny car with the dead engine. We were the new clothes with broken hearts. We were selfish and only seeking our own desires. What we needed to be doing was asking God how we could have a more fulfilling marriage. We finally got to that point and now work hard each year to keep it up.

Approaching the idea of maintenance is best when discussed early in the marriage, but it's not impossible to learn if you have been married for a long time. The best thing you can do is recognize the value and need of marriage maintenance and take steps to grow.

Here are 5 ways to help discuss marriage maintenance with your wife:

These can be done with or without your wife, but for the most beneficial results we highly recommend you discuss these questions with your wife now or later.

1) Discuss the need and value of maintaining your marriage

Whether you are about to be married, newlywed or have been married for years, take some time now to discuss the value of maintaining your marriage. Discuss what you and your wife think maintenance would look like and figure out how you can apply both of your views to your marriage. Take it a step further and write down your expectations.

2) Discuss how you want your marriage to look in 1 year

Talking to your wife about where you want your marriage to be a year from now can be powerful. If you are honest and mention things like being happy, getting into your first house or still being madly in love then you will need to discuss how you can achieve those goals. What will you both need to do in order to meet that one-year goal? Good communication or a good Church family, how about regular date nights? Share ideas with your spouse and make it a point to review those ideas at least once a month. Figure out the what, than figure out the how.

3) Discuss how you want your marriage to look in 5 years

Figuring out your one-year goal and achieving it is a strong start, but working towards some five-year goals can be even more intense. I like the idea of a longer-term goal because I believe it gives the marriage some strength and longevity. Too many marriages are ending in the first couple of years because, in my opinion and experience, they lack vision. They lack the necessary tools that could help them reach the five-year mark. The five-year goal could include having children, it could be maintaining an intimate relationship and it could involve helping each other reach specific personal goals. Whatever you may have in mind, talk about these goals now. Give yourself and your marriage some room to dream. Again, take things a step further and write these down. Review them every few months or at least at the beginning of each new year to help you maintain and stay on track.

4) Agree to stay available and open to marriage assistance

A lot of married couples, and in many cases just the husbands, don't like the idea of going to a marriage conference. I know the overall stigma and it goes something like this: "Marriage conferences are for those couples that are doing badly or need help." Well, I am here to break that myth and tell you that it is the complete opposite. Conferences are for couples who want to learn more about their marriage! They may have a strong marriage already but understand that there is still stuff they do not know. Couples who stay open and available to marriage assistance have and will maintain the strongest relationships. They don't have a hidden secret or potion, they are just willing to accept help and receive instruction. Are you open to instruction? Are you willing to take the lead in the coming months to find a way to learn something new about your marriage? Don't sit back and wait for your wife to do this because this is your territory! Find a class or conference this year and attend!

My wife and I have agreed that attending at least one marriage conference or group class is mandatory every year.

THE MARRIAGE ADVANCE

5) Keep Christ first in your own lives

Maintaining your marriage is important, but the best and most important aspect of a great marriage is each other's personal relationship with Jesus. If you take the time to walk with Christ while you are on your own and while you are away from your wife, you will always come back to her a stronger man. If you are willing to pray for yourself and your direction in life, you will provide your wife and family with more leadership than you could ever imagine. If you have never considered how your own relationship with Christ could be affecting your marriage, you need to do it now. Take a few moments to step back from your busy and important life, and consider these ideas. Are you personally living for Him? Are you asking Him to give you strength every day so that He will be there for you and your family on a consistent basis? These changes will make the biggest impact in your marriage. I guarantee it!

What Do You Do Now?

You keep going and set up a maintenance plan for yourself.

SET REMINDERS FOR YOURSELF

It's simple; you need to build a battle plan. You need to know what direction you are headed in your marriage and personal life. I personally have a phone reminder that goes off at the end of every month. I call it my

157

"Monthly Battle Plan" and it has gone off for almost four years now. The message that goes off for three days is simple but impactful. I made it and saved it to my calendar a couple months after my marriage almost collapsed. I wrote briefly about why I can't turn back to my old ways. I told myself to pray every day for my wife and for myself and I encouraged myself to keep on the path towards Jesus.

What steps can you take to remind yourself to keep fighting the good fight of faith? Real marriage maintenance requires real consistency.

BE ACCOUNTABLE TO OTHERS

I also became a lot more honest around some brothers of mine. They knew about some of my struggles and they said they would help me stay on the right track from here on out. If I needed to call for any reason, they would always try to make themselves available. To this day, there are at least two to four men that I could go to before I let the bottom fall out of my life or marriage.

Who are you accountable to? Real marriage maintenance requires real accountability.

PRAY

Don't make such a big deal out of how you pray. What you need to focus on is having a real conversation with God and often. A good friend once told me, "I don't pray a lot, but I do pray often." That quote has stuck with me ever since and I try to pray often. Since I have a long drive to work, I will intentionally turn off the radio and talk to God as though He is simply sitting in the seat next to me. I will ask for His thoughts and advice on whatever I am going through in life. Depending on the length of the drive, the conversation can go on for easily an hour or so. So, again, you don't have to be alone in some room, you can go to Him any time you need.

What steps can you take to establish a stronger prayer life? Real marriage maintenance requires a real prayer life.

Our Challenge to You

Here 5 easy ways to maintain your marriage for the years to come! Consider yourself challenged!

Attend a Marriage Class at Your Church

Be proactive and find out what classes are available for your marriage this week! Review the options and dates and write them down on the calendar. Make this a priority!

Attend a Marriage Conference

My wife and I have a goal of attending a marriage conference every year. We have made this a standard in our marriage that is not optional. Talk to some people at your Church this week and find out what conferences are coming up at your Church or in your general area. Although it might cost you a few bucks to attend, remember how much value it will add to your marriage.

Do a Devotional with Your Wife Every Week

I can admit that this is a tough one to achieve, but it is possible and the results are huge. With a devotional, you get to talk about a new marriage topic each week. This is great for your marriage and really helps when those unexpected events pop up. Getting a devotional is probably one of the cheapest options for marriage maintenance and the easiest.

Read through a Marriage Book Together

If reading a book with your wife sounds like a challenge, I encourage you to do it all the more. You can either read a chapter while you are apart or you can read through it together. The important part is that you read the chapter and then take some time to talk about the topics. You can visit the Resources page at Manturity.com to find some really good book options for your marriage.

Have a Monthly Date to Discuss Goals, Dreams and Matters of the Heart

I know life can get busy and even hectic at times, but it's critical that you maintain a great dating life with your wife. And just as I've mentioned in earlier paragraphs, don't wait for your wife to make the first move or set up the date, this is your territory and you need to be very intentional about it. I wouldn't let 2-3 months go by without taking your wife out to a nice dinner, a fun activity or movie or just a night on the town. This is what kept your dating life alive and it will help keep your marriage alive as well!

Take the initiative NOW to maintain your marriage and it will last a lifetime!

CHAPTER FIFTEEN

HOW TO ADVANCE IN YOUR MARRIAGE

By: Bryan & Jody

Don't advance in one area and assume you have the rest of the areas handled. Practice one skill, start and learn another!

QUESTION

So how do I advance in my marriage?

ANSWER

By reviewing, applying and maintaining the principals learned in the Word of God and in this book.

RELEVANT VERSES

"So I say to you: Ask and it will be given to you; seek and you will find; knock and the door will be opened to you. For everyone who asks receives; the one who seeks finds; and to the one who knocks, the door will be opened."
-Luke 11:9-10

"Rise up; this matter is in your hands. We will support you, so take courage and do it."
-Ezra 10:4

First off, let us start by saying great work! Your dedication to becoming a better man and husband will pay off more than you know when you complete the challenges laid out in this book. Without challenges, you're not going to grow; and if you don't grow, it will be exponentially harder to achieve the goals you have in life and in your marriage.

So the question remains, how will I advance in my marriage? Well, we believe digging into the Word of God and making it all the way through this book will immensely assist you in becoming a better man in your marriage. We strongly encourage you to review, apply and maintain the principals learned in this book and in the Word weekly!

As we bring the discussion of these important topics to a close, we want to challenge you in a few more ways. The principles you have learned and the work you have put into reading this book can't be left at the last page. So here are five ways we want to push forward your progress in your future.

You Advance in Your Marriage by Removing Excuses and Taking Action!

Consider these perspectives for a moment: Jody doesn't develop a sermon during the week and speak to the congregation on Sunday just to make the people in attendance become better people; no, he also becomes a better man and greater husband because of that work. By overcoming the distractions of the week and removing the easily fed excuses, he is able to impact those who attend his Church and his marriage.

Bryan has been maintaining Manturity.com for 5 years now! One of the top questions he gets asked is, "Why do you do it?" He'll tell you immediately it's how God called him to advance in his marriage after his near second divorce only 4 years into his marriage. Manturity has become his way of connecting with God on a daily basis and connecting with other men through each post, and it has created a way for him to keep Christ at the center of his marriage. Bryan has now learned that, in order to stay a strong man and in order to maintain a healthy marriage, he needed to remove all of his excuses and start taking action!

And now we want to challenge you! What excuses are holding you back? As Jody and Bryan can prove, you have a story. You also have a past that is holding you back and keeping you down. We get that, and we understand. But the past needs to be forgotten and forgiven. The past needs to be handed over to God and you must move on. What are some areas of your life in which you need to step up and take action?

You Advance In Your Marriage by Taking Action in the Areas You Feel Need the Most Work First

Jody took action by realizing one big thing, he was a spiritual sissy! He knew that this is where God was calling him to start taking action.

After giving his life to the Lord in 2003, the Holy Spirit took over in a way he would have never imagined. I began to fall in love with the word of God. Reading it on a daily basis and growing in the grace and knowledge of Jesus Christ.

This helped him immensely in his personal walk. But it didn't do a whole lot for his marriage at first. Once he began to apply what he was learning, everything changed. His love for God started to make him love others and that included his wife.

It wasn't that he didn't love her, he just didn't show her. Learning to love God should move you to love others. And that includes our wives. Our first ministry should be our wives!

By following the principles and teachings in the Bible, Jody's relationships all grew closer. Follow the Word of God and learn to love Him! That will help you be the husband you are called to be, selfless!

Bryan took action on his past. Even though he and his wife had tried to forgive each other, every little disagreement led to a much bigger fight that involved the major past issues. It wasn't until another man from Church told him that he realized only God could truly cover his marriage with forgiveness. It would only be through God that his marriage could move past the past. And with that information, the healing began. Bryan took on a 30-day challenge of waking up one hour early to read through the scriptures, specifically Proverbs, and pray. Not only did this provide a time of immense learning, but it provided a time to heal as a man. It gave him an opportunity to forgive his wife and himself for all of their past mistakes. A few months later, a few read books later, a marriage restored and the birth of Manturity.

So your challenge is to start taking action! What area of your life needs a major overhaul and needs it now? It could be similar to Jody or Bryan's story or it could be completely your own. Whatever it is, we want to encourage you to take action on it now. The best way to start is through prayer. Take an hour each morning to read and pray. Take some time to talk to your pastor or a good friend. Engage in the Man Up Gods Way app, available for free, and learn from the vast experience and community of engaged men. Do not wait! Take action in the area that needs the most work now, and work your way through some of the other ones later.

You Advance in Your Marriage by Being Accountable and Following Up

Confession in Jody's life opened of a form of communication and accountability that is hard to get other men to do. The more he read and applied the bible, the more the Holy Spirit would convict him to share his short comings; both with his wife and other men.

Jody believes that when the Holy Spirit prompts you to confess a sin, you need to share that with others. That kind of confession allows you to be open to the accountability of others. Sometimes he starts by sharing with another brother, then seeks the scripture, gets the sin out of his life and then shares it with his wife. As men, sometimes we need to share with someone who understands the struggle we go through. Not all women can. But eventually your wife needs to know and become your accountability partner. It grows you closer and unifies you both.

What really made Bryan successful moving forward was complete transparency with another Christian brother and staying in prayer daily. You can't do all of this alone! It doesn't matter who you are or how strong you think you are; it's extremely difficult to advance in your marriage by doing it alone. Bryan continued to speak to his pastor about his issues and was led by his pastor with very specific prayers. Accountability allowed Bryan to make calls to his brothers when he was in need the most. Whether it was when temptation was calling or when he felt the need to retaliate to his wife, he would call or text a brother and ask for immediate prayer. And on top of that, he still meets up with brothers often to personally discuss the issues in his life and in theirs. Accountability has been one of Bryan's biggest reasons for success and we know it can be for you too!

So stop making excuses and find an accountability partner today! Bryan found a mentor in a man at Church who God just kept pointing out to him. He had to take the lead in talking to him, and we want to encourage you to do the same. Have you seen that man? Have you briefly spoken to a man you thought would make a great mentor? You need to ask! Remove excuses and take action! Seeking accountability could produce a relationship that could last a lifetime. You just need to take that first step.

You Advance in Your Marriage by Joining the Community

When it comes down to it men, there are plenty of powerful ways to grow in your walk with Christ and in your marriage. You must choose to take action and join a community. A community can be found by joining a local Church. And if you're at a local Church, it could mean becoming more involved with the men there. Community can be found online through groups, pages and more.

Jody and Bryan have partnered to bring you the Man Up Gods Way app. This app has over 15,000 men who lock shields together every day to read, learn, share and grow on every possible topic. Our Hurdles section is our most powerful part of the app. This section allows for anonymous sharing about your struggles, pains, addictions and more; and there are real men there ready to share their experience and offer their prayers and advice. There are monthly challenges that will encourage you to get out of your comfort zone and engage in something real. And there are powerful resources shared every week to help you grow in your marriage, faith and manhood.

Real community with other real men is out there, my brothers. As you close the pages of this book, please consider staying active in some kind of community with other men who will challenge you each and every day!

You Advance in Your Marriage by Not Letting This Training Go

We encourage you to review and change your habits as you move forward. Everything you have learned in this book and all of the challenges offer you real change, but you must be ready to change your habits.

As you accomplish and start to maintain one major area needed for improvement suggested in this book, we strongly encourage you to start working on your next one. Don't advance in one area and assume you have the rest of the areas handled. Practice one skill, start and learn another!

We challenge you to share what you're working on with your wife. There are many changes discussed over the course of this book and, as you start to change, your wife might begin to ask questions. Open up to your wife and let her know what you're doing. Let her know that you're seeking accountability and that you're getting up early to read the scriptures. By doing this, you are starting to set a strong example. No, she may not believe you at first and you can't let this affect what you're doing. Stay strong, stay consistent and keep working towards your first goal. She will notice and love you for it soon!

Don't stop praying! As you embark on each new journey and challenge in this book, do not forget to pray first. Pray that God will open your heart to hear what He has to say. Pray for direction as you look to improve multiple parts of your life and marriage. And don't forget to pray for your marriage. Don't ask for what you want, instead ask that God's Will be done in it!

We pray daily that God will help you advance in your marriage every day!

Do you know someone who needs to hear this message? If so, consider giving them your copy. Or, please consider buying and sending a copy to them today. Pray over that decision and follow up. God bless!

<u>NOTES</u>

PRAYER LIST

<u>YOUR PERSONAL MAINTENANCE PLAN</u>